THE PENTLAND HILLS

A WALKER'S GUIDE

About the Author

Susan Falconer began walking in the Pentlands in her early teens. After graduating with a degree in geography from St Andrews University she began a management career in the health service in London. Despite being many miles from her native country, she returned regularly to walk and cycle in Scotland. She trained as a teacher and became senior tutor in ecology and geography for the Field Studies Council in Epping Forest. Susan returned to Scotland to take up the post of countryside education officer for the Scottish Agricultural College, before becoming a countryside ranger with the Pentland Hills Ranger Service in 1995. She enjoys hill walking, cycling and wildlife, and contributes articles to the *Pentland Beacon* and other publications. This is her first guidebook.

THE PENTLAND HILLS

A WALKER'S GUIDE

by
Susan Falconer

2 POLICE SQUARE, MILNTHORPE, CUMBRIA LA7 7PY
www.cicerone.co.uk

First edition 2007
Reprinted 2008 (with amendments)
ISBN-13: 978-1-85284-494-3
© Susan Falconer 2007

DEDICATION

This book is dedicated to the memory of my mother, Evelyn, who allowed me the freedom to explore the hills.

Acknowledgements

Many people have helped me along the way, but I would particularly like to thank the following: Michael Jones for sharing his knowledge, friendship and books with me; John Stirling for encouragement and checking the routes; Roger Oakes for help in an area of the hills less familiar; Jonathan Williams, Hazel Clarke and Liz Inman for making it all happen; Kym Martindale for grammatical assistance; Jenny Hargreaves for moral support, and all at the Pentland Hills Ranger Service. The hills are in good hands.

Advice to Readers

Readers are advised that while every effort is taken by the author to ensure the accuracy of this guidebook, changes can occur which may affect the contents. It is advisable to check locally on transport, accommodation, shops, etc., but even rights of way can be altered. Paths can be affected by forestry work, landslip or changes of ownership.

The author would welcome information on any updates and changes sent through the publishers.

Front cover: Walkers setting off up Turnhouse Hill (Walk 22)

CONTENTS

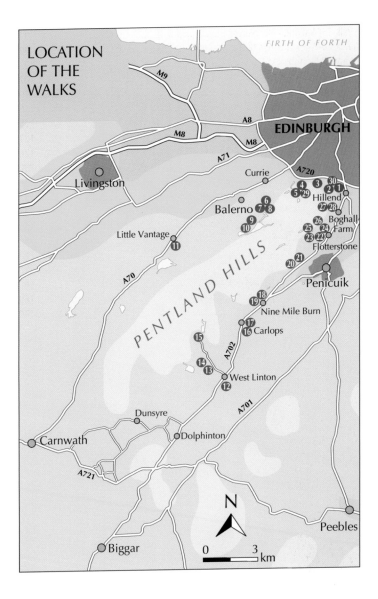

LOCATION
OF THE
WALKS

Overflow at Glencorse Reservoir (Walk 24) (PHRS)

INTRODUCTION

'The Pentland Hills are homely and friendly hills; they lie near the bounds of our city habitation, and frequent visiting begets an intimacy and friendship that is real and lasting. The most outlying parts may be reached in the course of a day's walk, and places of silence, where none will intrude, are easily accessible.' Will Grant's words from his 1927 book *The Call of the Pentlands* are as relevant today as when they were first written. The Pentland Hills comprise a rich tapestry of landscapes and landforms, all neatly packaged within an area easily accessible from Scotland's majestic capital city. Although principally a grass- and heather-clad, softly rounded hill range, the hills reward further exploration by revealing stunning summit vistas, quiet waterside strolls, deeply incised rocky valleys and wooded walks, as well as a fascinating natural and cultural heritage.

The Pentlands are well known to the people of Edinburgh; even for those who have not actually visited them, they form a familiar backdrop to city life. This hill range – Robert Louis Stevenson's 'hills of home' – arouses strong feelings, and on their return to Edinburgh, either by road, rail or air, many people regard their first glimpse of the Pentlands as confirmation of finally arriving home.

The Pentland Hills run southwest from Edinburgh towards Biggar, covering an area of 210 sq km, and their generally rounded appearance is the result of sculpting by glaciers and meltwater. They reach a maximum height of 579m at Scald Law, although most lie between 400m and 550m in height.

Approximately 90 sq km in the northern sector of the Pentlands was designated a regional park (the Pentland Hills Regional Park) in 1986, with the aim of acknowledging and safeguarding the landscape, wildlife and recreational value of this important location. The regional park benefits from a ranger service, which assists land managers and visitors by maintaining the path infrastructure, providing waymarking and interpretation, and giving advice on responsible access. The path network is well signposted, and a diverse range of cultural and natural heritage adds interest to the scenery.

The Pentlands offer good variety for the walker, with the excellent path system, interesting but not too rugged terrain, and proximity to civilisation adding up to a superb introduction to hill walking in Scotland. These hills are especially suitable for beginners (Walks 1 to 7), although the longer and more remote routes (Walks 11,

13, 14 and 15) in the southern end, which is a more open, exposed and remote landscape, with less obvious waymarking and more challenging navigation on some routes, should satisfy the more seasoned hiker. Walks 19, 20, 24 and 25 should also appeal to more experienced walkers. A basic level of navigational skills is required, but none of the routes should cause any wayfinding difficulties.

My approach to writing this guidebook is to imagine that I, as a countryside ranger, am taking the reader on a walk. It reflects what I would point out and note as a ranger on patrol, with the addition of snippets of research that I have found interesting along the way.

The Pentlands are *included* in many walking guides about the Lothians and Scotland, but to my knowledge there has, so far, been no walking guide dedicated solely to the Pentland Hills. This shortage of comprehensive walking guides led to the writing of this book.

APPROACHES AND ACCOMMODATION

The Pentlands is one of the most accessible hill ranges in Scotland, well served by roads on all sides: the A720 Edinburgh city bypass to the north; the A70 Lanark road to the west; the A721 to the south; the A702 (T) Biggar road to the east. This network of roads means that the hills are

Approaching Scald Law from the Kirk Road End (Walk 21)

Loganlee Dam and Carnethy (Walk 29)

readily accessible by car or bicycle, although bus services are variable. The northern end is well served by public transport from Edinburgh, e.g. Lothian Buses number 4 to Hillend (Walks 1, 2, 30), number 10 to Torphin and Bonaly (Walks 4, 5, 29), and number 44 to Balerno (Walks 9 and 10), all leaving from Princes Street in the city centre. A regular service from central Edinburgh to Dumfries, via MacEwen's Coach Services number 100, uses the A702 (Walks 12, 16, 17, 22, 23, 24 and 25).

A comprehensive leaflet entitled *How to Get to the Pentland Hills by Bus*, with a map and route suggestions, is available from the Pentland Hills Ranger Service. It can be downloaded from www.pentlandhills.org, or is available from the visitor centres at Flotterstone or Harlaw. Check with local operators for the latest service information, or phone Traveline 0870 608 2608.

For those who need accommodation, Edinburgh offers a great choice – campsites, hostels, bed and breakfasts, guesthouses and hotels are all within easy reach. Penicuik, West Linton and Lanark are alternatives, and www.visitscotland.com has details of accommodation for all these locations.

CHOOSING A WALK

The walks described are a personal selection, chosen to give a flavour of the hills at their best. The Pentlands

Heading off up Turnhouse Hill (Walk 25)

do not cover a vast tract of land, and inevitably routes cross and cover some of the same ground, but every walk is different in character, and the experience of walking it is influenced by weather, mood, companions and so on. (For each walk there is a brief description, at the beginning, summarising its character.)

As far as possible, the routes are circular, as this reduces the need for additional transport, and reflects the fact that the majority of walkers (myself included) prefer not to retrace their steps. For some walks you need to retrace your steps for a short way, back to the start point, but none is linear. Optional links with other routes in the book are included, to lengthen some walks (e.g. Walks 2, 4, 6, 12 and 16), and informative 'points of interest' are found throughout.

The walks are presented in order as follows: starting at Hillend, at the northern end of the Pentlands, nearest Edinburgh, then moving southwest along the A70 down as far as Little Vantage, and finally skipping across to West Linton and back up the A702 to return to the beginning.

The lack of routes along the A70 between Harperrig and Carnwath is a reflection of the lack of public transport, few safe and accessible parking areas, and a shortage of good walking routes with interesting features along the way.

ACCESS RIGHTS AND RESPONSIBILITIES

The Land Reform (Scotland) Act 2003 was passed by the Scottish parliament in 2003 and enacted through the Scottish Outdoor Access Code in

February 2005. The Act gives everyone the right to be on most land or water for recreation, providing they act responsibly. Acting responsibly means: using stiles to cross fences; leaving gates as you found them; keeping your dog under control; respecting the needs of land managers and other users. There is a long tradition of access by walkers to the Pentlands, and most land managers are tolerant and understanding of responsible recreation.

The Pentlands are used extensively for sheep farming, water catchment, arable crops, military training and game shooting.

Sheep

The lambing and tupping (when the male tupps are mating with the ewes) seasons are particularly sensitive times of year. Lambing usually takes place between March and May, and tupping in November. Dogs must not be taken into fields with lambs (or calves), and must be kept under close control in fields with other animals.

Grouse Shooting

Grouse shoots may take place in August and September. The line of the drive is usually obvious, and well managed and signposted by the estate, but do be extra vigilant during these months.

Military Training

A sector of the northern Pentlands from Dreghorn through to Castlelaw is used by the army for training. Live firing takes place on the ranges near Castlelaw farm and is clearly marked and signposted. Dry training may take place in the sector at any other time, but again is signposted. Please be aware of this, especially on Walks 5, 23, 25, 26, 28, 29 and 30. Responsible walking access is not usually affected by military training, but please obey any signage or instructions for your own safety.

Wildlife

The routes described in this book are mainly on paths and tracks, making for easier walking, and minimising disturbance to wildlife. Walking *off* the path may disturb ground-nesting birds, such as curlew, skylark and red grouse, so please take care where you are walking, especially during the March to July nesting season. Check for details at www.outdooraccess-scotland.com

WEATHER

The Pentlands can be enjoyed in all seasons – crisp winter days when time and light are short, warm days in spring or summer, or bright autumn mornings. In general they are not subject to extremes of weather, and enjoy a benign climate. Most weather systems affecting the range come from the west, bringing fronts of wet and windy conditions, and the tops can be very windy in exposed areas. Snowfall tends to last no more than a few days (cross-country skiing has only been possible on a handful of days in the past few years), but electrical storms can be a hazard on exposed ground, in which case a speedy retreat to lower down is recommended.

Wet weather means that streams and rivers can rapidly become hazardous to cross. Walks 1, 8, 21 and 23 do *not* involve crossing water, but bridges, spillways and dams will be encountered on all the other walks. Be aware that things can change, however, including the condition of structures, particularly after adverse weather. Be especially vigilant after heavy rain or snow melt, and if in doubt, *do not cross*.

A useful website that offers a hills- and mountain-orientated weather forecast is www.mwis.org.uk.

EQUIPMENT

The range of equipment available to outdoor enthusiasts is quite staggering. I've seen people equipped to tackle the north face of the Eiger rather than Turnhouse Hill (Walk 8), as well as those whose footwear and clothing can only be described as inadequate for the weather and terrain they were about to attempt. In general, a good pair of walking boots, appropriate warm, waterproof clothing – or a hat and sunscreen, depending on the weather – plus a rucksack with food, drink, map, compass and guidebook, are all that is needed. (In 1927, Will Grant, author of *The Call of the Pentlands*, recommended a good thick Harris tweed suit and a pair of strong boots with tackets (hobnails) for walks in winter. Tweed and tackets have been replaced by more modern materials, but the principle is the same.) (Note: mobile phone coverage in the Pentlands is patchy, with many areas of poor or non-existent reception.)

FOLLOWING A ROUTE

Maps
The maps in this guide are taken from the Ordnance Survey Landranger (1:50,000) series. The information box at the start of each walk gives details of the relevant OS Landranger and Explorer (1:25,000) maps for that walk. For all the walks in this guidebook you will need the following:
- Landranger 65 (Falkirk and West Lothian)
- Landranger 66 (Edinburgh)
- Landranger 72 (Upper Clyde Valley)
- Explorer 344 (Pentland Hills)

Map references beginning NT and followed by six figures will be found

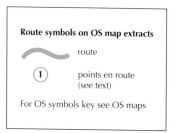

Route symbols on OS map extracts

route

(1)   points en route
(see text)

For OS symbols key see OS maps

in the walk instructions. These are included to locate the exact start point of each route and to assist with navigation along the way.

Times

An approximate time needed to complete the route is also given in the information box. These times have been calculated using Naismith's Rule of 4km/hour, plus 1 minute for every 10m of ascent. Some walkers will be faster, others slower, and the times do not allow for lunch breaks or other stoppages.

The information box also includes: **Distance**, **Ascent**, **Start/ Finish** and a short **walk summary**.

Route Description

The main route description describes the ground covered, and has been thoroughly tried and tested. The numbered paragraphs correspond to the numbers along the line of the route on the map. (Be aware that things can change, however – trees are felled, footbridges become unsafe, and land management is ongoing – so be prepared for discrepancies between the route description and what you encounter on the ground.)

GEOLOGY AND LANDSCAPE

The Pentlands landscape owes its distinctive profile to the hardness of the 400-million-year-old volcanic rock, lava and ash of the Devonian period.

The heart of the Pentlands is formed from the folded sedimentary rocks of the Silurian age (435 million

Geology at the Howe (Walk 8)

years), mainly marine shales and sandstones. This core is only exposed at three places: North Esk, Green Cleuch (e.g. Walk 8) and Loganlea. But it is the rocks of the succeeding Old Red Sandstone period (400 to 350 million years old) that have contributed to the form of the Pentlands we see today. After a period of erosion, coarse conglomerates and sandstones were laid down, and at this time volcanic activity also increased, and lavas and tuffs (volcanic ash) were deposited.

The rocks are classified according to the minerals they contain. Basalts and andesites are richly charged with iron oxides such as haematite, and are seen in the characteristic dark-red screes and outcrops found beside the lower part of Flotterstone Glen road (e.g. Walk 24). Rhyolytes and trachytes tend to be pink or pale orange in colour. Rhyolyte can be seen on the summit of Caerketton Hill (e.g. Walk 1) and trachytes are best seen on Torduff Hill (e.g. Walk 4). Tuffs, pale in colour and often containing distinct fragments of other rocks, can be found on the summit of Carnethy Hill (e.g. Walk 21).

The rocks of the Upper Old Red Sandstone age are found around West and East Cairn Hills (e.g. Walks 11 and 15). Earth movements during the Lower Carboniferous period created the Pentland Fault (the A702 follows the line of the fault), which separates

Mendick Hill from the Roman road (Walk 13)

the Pentlands from the Midlothian coalfield.

The rounded profiles of the hills, the deposits of boulder clay and striated (scratched) rock surfaces, are evidence that an ice sheet scoured the Pentlands. In the last two million years, warmer spells between ice ages caused the ice to melt, and vast quantities of meltwater cut out channels to lower ground. Green Cleuch (e.g. Walk 9) and the area to the west of Carlops (e.g. Walk 16) are excellent examples of these meltwater channels.

The hard, volcanic rocks have been used to construct cairns, dwellings, dykes and roads around the hills. The shape of the land, with its valleys and relatively non-porous rock, has been well utilised for water catchment.

To discover more about the geology of the Pentlands, try www.edinburghgeolsoc.org.

CULTURAL HERITAGE

There is an impressive range of archaeological sites and remains in the Pentlands. These include the early Bronze Age cairn on Carnethy Hill (e.g. Walk 8), the souterrain (an underground chamber or passage) at Castlelaw (e.g. Walk 5), and forts at Clubbiedean (e.g. Walk 4), Braidwood and Lawhead (e.g. Walk 22). Other places, such as Cairns Castle (Walk 11) and the site of the Battle of Rullion Green (Walk 22), are testament to some of the area's more

turbulent times. More recently, Robert Louis Stevenson and Sir Walter Scott have been inspired to base stories and characters on the area's past events (see Walks 2, 4 and 28, for example).

PLACE NAMES AND DIALECT WORDS

Place Names

Today, a place name may seem merely a convenient label to attach to a location, but when it was originally applied to that place, the name must have had a particular significance. Place names can give us an insight into the past and those who populated it, and included in this book is background to some of the place names in the Pentlands.

Place names are evidence of the languages used by the succession of different peoples who lived in the Lothians. Celtic, the language of the early Iron Age British Celts, survives in Pentland names such *caep*, 'pointed hill', as in West Kip (Walk 3). The British Celts saw the Romans arrive and were largely trading allies. In the 7th century the area was conquered by the Northumbrian Angles, and Anglian is reflected in *laecc*, 'boggy stream' (Walk 5). Gaelic names appear later, around the 10th century, as a result of political change. A Pentland example is *cloch mead*, 'the stone at the middle of the pass' (Walk 4). From the 11th century to the 18th century estate and farming names began to dominate, although they often reflect earlier origins.

I have drawn heavily on Stuart Harris's *The Place Names of Edinburgh, Their Origins and History* (see bibliography), and some research was undertaken by the Scottish Place-Name Society, so if this is an area of interest for you, it may be worth looking at www.st-and.ac.uk/institutes/sassi/spns.

Dialect Words

A number of words in the text may be unfamiliar to readers, so a brief glossary is included as Appendix 3. These are local terms used for places and wildlife. The word 'cleuch' (or sometimes 'cleugh', used chiefly by map makers) is used often and means a narrow valley. 'Bealach' is a pass or saddle between two hills, sometimes termed a col. I have used the local phrase 'drystane dyke' to describe a wall built without mortar.

'Peewit', 'whaup' and 'laverock' (lapwing, curlew and skylark respectively) are birds you will probably encounter on a walk in the Pentlands. Personally, I like these names, and encourage their continued use.

OLD MAPS

The British Isles are very well served in terms of maps. The practise of making maps stretches back centuries, with a variety of reasons for their production – military, land holding, legal and fiscal, and so on – and the late 19th century saw a rise in the use of maps as an aid to walking and recreation. The earliest maps referred to in this book are: Adair's maps of Midlothian and West Midlothian, from 1682; A and M Armstrong's Map of the Three Lothians, surveyed in 1773; Roy's 1753 Military Survey of Scotland; Knox's 1812 Edinburgh and Its Environs. After this the Ordnance Survey provides the basis for today's cartography, with foundations laid by the Ordnance Survey six-inch maps from 1852 onwards.

The National Library of Scotland has an excellent digital library of maps, and their website is www.nls.uk.

PREVIOUS PENTLANDS GUIDEBOOKS

A number of guidebooks have been written about the Pentland Hills, mainly in the last century, and they are an eclectic mix. George Reith's *The Breezy Pentlands* (1910) is a lovely blend of heritage and walking routes, with humour laced throughout. *Pentland Walks with Their Literary and Historical Associations* (Robert Cochrane, 1908) describes a series of routes combined with cultural background and details of the literary connections of the hills (this book formed the basis of DG Moir's *Pentland Walks, Their Literary and Historical Associations*, published in 1977). William Anderson's *The Pentland Hills* (1926) – not written as a guidebook but as an appreciation – makes interesting reading.

Probably the best known of the Pentlands guidebooks is Will Grant's *The Call of the Pentlands* (1927), and another of Grant's books, *Pentland Days and Country Ways* (1934), is an anthology of stories about and reflections on the hills.

Swanston Cottage (Walk 2)

The publication of these books reflected the growing interest in walking and the countryside amongst ordinary people during the 20th century, as more leisure time became available and travelling became easier.

The early 1990s saw a further two Pentlands books published: *The Pentlands' Pocket Book* by Albert Morris and James Bowman in 1990, and Jim Crumley's *Discovering the Pentland Hills* a year later. Ian Munro's *The Birds of the Pentland Hills* also makes fascinating reading, reflecting the changing weather, the character of the people, and Ian Munro's own love of the area.

LITERARY CONNECTIONS WITH THE PENTLAND HILLS

The Pentlands have provided inspiration for many writers, and Cochrane's *Pentland Walks with Their Literary and Historical Associations* and Moir's *Pentland Walks, Their Literary and Historical Associations* both describe these connections. Allan Ramsay based his pastoral comedy *The Gentle Shepherd* in the area around Carlops (Walks 16 and 17). Sir Walter Scott and Robert Louis Stevenson walked the northern Pentlands extensively, and Walk 2 covers much of the area explored by Stevenson. (The poets Wilfred Owen and Siegfried Sassoon, both evacuated to Craiglockhart Hospital in 1917, also walked in these hills.) (See bibliography, Appendix 2, for details of the above titles.)

PROTECTING AND ENJOYING THE HILLS

The Pentland Hills have long been a destination for people seeking recreation in the countryside. Well over a century ago, in 1883, the Scottish Rights of Way and Access Society began two years of negotiation with landowners and surveying of paths, and in 1885 inaugural signposts were erected on most Pentland paths. The society produced the first walking guidebook, with a copy presented to

Bonaly Reservoir from Harbour Hill (Walk 4)

each Pentland landowner, and a further 300 to the Edinburgh Trades Council – for distribution amongst working men 'in order that healthful enjoyment and recreation afforded by the rights of way across the hills should be better known'. The society continues its invaluable work today.

With improved and increased access, however, came an increase in problems – with litter, for example. In *The Pentland Hills*, William Anderson complained, back in 1926 '...there is nothing more offensive than, on arriving...to find the outflow choked with paper or cardboard boxes, and the ground littered with orange and banana skins, broken bottles, and such like' (although his suggestion for hiding litter in molehills or under heather bushes is not acceptable now). On 24 May 1932 the *Scotsman* reported that the Victoria Day holiday

saw thousands trekking to the hills, the lonely spaces being invaded from an early hour and traffic to Flotterstone Bridge (Walk 23) exceptionally heavy.

Recognition of the Pentlands' role in Edinburgh's recreation activities, and the need for protection of the hills, has been noted for decades. Letters to the *Scotsman* in November 1945 suggested that the Pentlands become the United Kingdom's first national park, dedicated to the memory of those who gave their lives for their country in the Second World War. But it was not until the late 1960s that the Pentlands were considered for legislative protection under the Countryside (Scotland) Act 1967, and the idea of designating the area a regional park was first mooted. After much debate, eventually leading to a public enquiry, on 12 September

1986 the Secretary of State for Scotland confirmed that 9158 hectares of the Pentland Hills was designated a regional park.

The act of designating this area a regional park served to acknowledge the beauty of the landscape, the importance of the wildlife, and the recreational value of this working area. As a regional park, the objective is to retain and enhance the essential character of the hills as a place for peaceful enjoyment of the countryside.

The role of the Pentland Hills Ranger Service is to ensure the integration of responsible access with farming, and the other land uses in the hills. This is done through maintaining the path network, providing waymarking and signage, staffing visitor centres at Flotterstone and Harlaw, producing maps and leaflets about responsible enjoyment, and patrolling to be a practical presence for visitors and land managers alike.

For information on Scotways and the Pentland Hills Regional Park, visit www.scotways.org and www.pentlandhills.org

WILDLIFE

The varied habitats of the Pentlands give rise to a rich diversity of wildlife.

Heather moorland is home to **red grouse**, the **merlin**, **mountain hare**, **emperor moth** and **green hairstreak butterfly**. 'Muirburn' – the deliberate burning of areas of mature heather to create a mosaic of differing ages and varying heights of heather – benefits many species. The new shoots and variety of structures in a well-managed moor provide food and cover for birds, mammals and insects.

The many reservoirs in the Pentlands are especially good for wildfowl. Westwater (e.g. Walk 14) is a Ramsar site (a wetland of international importance), especially significant for

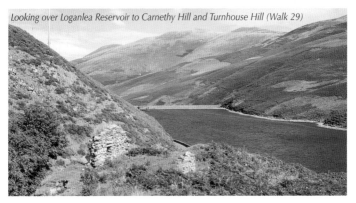

Looking over Loganlea Reservoir to Carnethy Hill and Turnhouse Hill (Walk 29)

thousands of **pink-footed geese** in the winter. Threipmuir (e.g. Walk 7) has **mallard**, **teal**, **whooper swan** and **great crested grebe**, and North Esk has a noisy colony of **black-headed gulls**. Smaller ponds support colourful insects such as the **large red damselfly** and **common hawker dragonfly**, as well as **common frogs** and **palmate** and **smooth newts**.

Grasslands are home to **brown hares**, **short-eared owls**, the **common shrew** and **meadow brown butterfly**.

The Pentlands are not heavily wooded – there are a few conifer plantations, and the 19th-century shelter belts and woodlands surrounding reservoirs support birds such as the **willow warbler**, **crossbill**, **goldcrest** and **sparrowhawk**.

Fungi are often overlooked, or in some cases destroyed by people, but they play a vital role in recycling nutrients in a woodland or grassland. They are a fascinating group of organisms in their own right, and to discover more about them, visit www.britmycolsoc.org.uk

Patches of gorse scrub are good places to find **stonechats** and **whinchats**, as well as **robins** and **wrens**, and rocky screes are the haunt of **common lizards**, which bask in the sun.

Bogs and marsh are where plants and animals specially adapted to their surroundings can be found. Insectivorous plants such as **roundleaved sundew** and **butterwort** grow on damp ground, and obtain essential nutrients from the flies and beetles they trap.

There is usually some wildlife interest at any time of year on the walks described.

Cauliflower fungus at base of Scots pine (Walk 6)

WALK 1
A Capital View

Distance	5.5km
Ascent	390m
Time	2 hours
Maps	Ordnance Survey Landranger 66 or
	Ordnance Survey Explorer 344
Start/Finish	Hillend car park NT249669

1 Begin at the **Hillend** car park next to the bus terminus at the entrance to the Midlothian Snowsports Centre. There is a waymarker post here – follow the sign indicating Capital View Walk.

Make your way uphill on a broad path over grassy slopes, then through sparsely wooded areas with bracken, gorse and trees, for about 600m. Follow the Capital View waymarkers and finger posts from this point.

Keep walking uphill on a path through Hillend Country Park to reach an open grassy knoll at NT245672, near the ski runs. There is a wooden bench here so you can sit and admire the views over the city and beyond.

A short, and in places steep, walk rewarded with magnificent views across the city and surrounding hill ranges. Excellent on a crisp winter's day when time and light are short.

Juniper berries

On the top of the knoll are the faint remains of a **fort**, possibly Iron Age. All that is visible of its rampart is a low mound and a stretch of ditch and bank, but with imagination the structures that would have been here 2000 years ago can be visualised.

Descend the knoll on a path to the west, and at another signpost indicating Caerketton, cross the fence using a stile and follow the path as it zigzags up the bulk of **Caerketton Hill**. Climb up onto the ridge, ascending 100m in 500m.

The shrubs in the wooden enclosures to your right on the way up Caerketton Hill are **junipers**, one of three conifers native to Scotland. Juniper is scarce in the Pentlands and bushes are scattered (they may once have been plentiful, but there is some dispute over this – see Malcolm Cant's *Villages of Edinburgh: An Illustrated Guide Vol. II*). To help re-establish juniper in the hills, the Pentland Hills Regional Park with Defence Estates, Forest Research and BTCV (Scotland) are undertaking a programme of growing-on cuttings and berries to plant in other suitable places. Berries, which do not form on the juniper bushes until the bushes are eight years old, are used to flavour gin, as well as making a peppery seasoning for venison or duck.

2 There is a tumbled-down cairn on Caerketton Hill, possibly of Bronze Age origin (see also Walk 27). Enjoy the views over Edinburgh and beyond, perhaps agreeing with Lord Cockburn that this is one of the three finest viewpoints in Scotland (along with Ben Lomond by Loch Lomond and Dumyat in the Ochil Hills, north of Stirling).

Continue on a path along the ridge until you start to descend rocky slopes to a bealach (pass) between Caerketton and **Byerside Hill**, at NT231664. (A stile and path leading downhill to your left drop down to Boghall Glen, which you could use to link with Walk 27, and return to Hillend via Boghall Plantation.) Continue over Byerside Hill on a muddy path, and then up the grassy slope of **Allermuir Hill** to its viewpoint indicator and trig pillar at 493m.

The original indicator on **Allermuir Hill** was presented to the National Trust for Scotland in 1963 by Arthur Russell, the Trust's law officer. The indicator also includes a reminder that the northern slopes of the Pentlands are protected by a conservation agreement between the landowner, Major Henry Trotter, and the National Trust for Scotland.

The viewpoint indicator on Allermuir summit

3 Descend Allermuir Hill by the same route over Byerside Hill and return to the bealach below Caerketton. Instead of climbing back over Caerketton (although this is an option), take a grassy path that goes north, leading downhill. This path divides lower down, and you should follow it as it cuts to the right across the lower slopes of Caerketton, overlooking the **T Wood** towards Hillend, and passing **Muilieputchie** (NT236666 – not shown on the OS 1:50,000 map).

The unusual name **Muilieputchie** is found on the OS 6in to 1 mile map of 1852, and according to S Harris's *The Place Names of Edinburgh, Their Origins and History* (see bibliography), may be British *moel* or Gaelic *maoile*, meaning 'hill brow', and Gaelic *poiteag*, a 'pit' or 'well', or British *puth*. However this is disputed, and the name may have a Scots root, *moolie* meaning 'mouldy', and *pooch* meaning 'pocket', hence 'a damp hollow'.

Viewed from Edinburgh the **T Wood** resembles a letter T, but in fact it is in the shape of a Maltese cross. It was planted in 1766 by Henry Trotter, to commemorate a member of the Trotter family of Mortonhall who had fallen in battle. The wood is mainly of beech trees, which cast a lot of shade, so there is very little understorey of other plants.

4 The path continues alongside the fence overlooking **Lothianburn Golf Course**. Keep on this path until you reach a gate and a path at the side of the plantation of conifers on the west side of the ski runs. Take this path steeply downhill and emerge at the ski centre upper car park. Head downhill, picking up a path that runs parallel to the road and return to the start.

WALK 2
In Stevenson's Footsteps

Distance	6km
Ascent	315m
Time	2 hours
Maps	Ordnance Survey Landranger 66 or
	Ordnance Survey Explorer 344
Start/Finish	Swanston car park NT240674

1 Leave the small car park below **Swanston** village by a path that winds through some trees and crosses a small burn by a metal bridge. Just as you emerge from the trees there is a signpost indicating Allermuir, Hillend and Lothianburn, so follow the direction finger

A walk with many historical connections, particularly with Robert Louis Stevenson. The whitewashed cottages of Swanston, T Wood and the Reindeer Cave all add to the interest. (This route can be lengthened by joining Walk 30 at Capelaw Hill – add 8km, 60m of ascent and 2 hours 10 minutes.)

for **Allermuir**. Walk uphill on a stony track, passing a small group of stone cottages to your left, overlooking a communal green. These date from the late 19th century and originally housed farmworkers.

Thatched cottages at Swanston village

There is a bench on either side of the track, one with an inscription to Edwin Muir, the poet and novelist, the other to a former resident, John Roe.

Continue on the track up to Swanston village, passing the old schoolhouse on the right. The early-18th-century whitewashed thatched cottages are a pretty scene, perhaps more reminiscent of an English village. ◀ Go through the kissing gate ahead and follow the path up amongst gorse along the side of the golf course – ahead are **T Wood** and **Caerketton screes**. Continue uphill, crossing a sleeper bridge, and here take the path to the left and go through another kissing gate. Continue further uphill through gorse towards Caerketton.

2 Keep on heading uphill alongside T Wood and the golf course until you reach a SRWS signpost indicating Allermuir (this area is marked on the OS Explorer map as Muilieputchie). Follow the Allermuir path over the knoll to a wet area.

3 Just beyond the wet area the path divides, so stay to the right, again climbing uphill to the northwest of **Byerside Hill**.

4 The path continues on up to **Allermuir Hill**, where there is an Ordnance Survey triangulation pillar and a viewpoint. After enjoying the views (on a clear day) descend quite steeply to your right on a path to reach an obvious stony track at NT223660. (There is the option of lengthening this walk considerably by linking with Walk 30, to ascend Capelaw Hill, and return to Swanston via Bonaly, Torduff Reservoir and Dreghorn.)

5 Take the stony track north down **Howden Glen** until you reach a stone building, **Green Craig Cistern**. ▶

Green Craig Cistern was constructed in 1790 and engraved on the door lintel is 'Edinburgh Thomas Elder Praefect MDCCIXC'. Thomas Elder of Forneth was lord provost of Edinburgh from 1788 to 1790.

> To the east of Green Craig Cistern, on the northern slopes of Allermuir Hill, is a rocky outcrop at 260m. It was here, in 1886, in a cleft in the rocks known as the **Reindeer Cave**, that a number of animal bones were found by RA Macfie, owner of Dreghorn Castle and Redford House. Most of the bones were reindeer, but there were also wolf, fox and horse. Speculation as to the identity of the carnivore that left them here has ranged from a hyena to a wolf.

The infant Howden Burn – 'the burn of the howe den' (from holh *meaning hollow and* den *meaning valley) – rises in Howden Glen.*

T Wood with Edinburgh beyond

6 From Green Craig Cistern take the path to the right that skirts the foot of the hill, passing the aptly named **Smithy Cleuch** (from the Scots *smailly*, meaning 'narrow'), and keeping by the plantations until you reach the path that threads along by **Long Plantation** at NT230676. This point is about 1km from Green Craig Cistern.

7 Go over a stile (or through the gate) straight ahead onto a wide track, which tucks in behind **Torgeith Knowe**, and some gas installation buildings on your left and a golf course on your right. Follow the track until you come to a large whitewashed house to your left, set in mature gardens – this is **Swanston Cottage**. From Swanston Cottage continue past a small lodge house on your left and the livery yard on your right. Return to the car park by walking past some converted farm buildings (now offices) and turning right when you reach the road, slightly up the hill.

The Reindeer Cave at Green Craig

Swanston Cottage, and indeed the area around the hamlet, has strong associations with Robert Louis Stevenson. The house was built in the late 18th century as a general meeting place for the Edinburgh city fathers. A second storey was added in 1835, the thatched roof replaced with slate, and bow windows built. Thomas Stevenson, Robert Louis' father, took the summer tenancy of the house in 1867. The cottage and surroundings became the setting for many of Stevenson's novels and poems, including *St Ives* and *The Pentland Rising*.

WALK 3
Hill, Moor and Wood

Distance	7km (including a circuit of the reservoir)
Ascent	225m
Time	2 hours
Maps	Ordnance Survey Landranger 66 or Ordnance Survey Explorer 344
Start/Finish	Dreghorn car park NT228679

1 Start from **Dreghorn** car park, just off the A720 at Dreghorn junction (NT228679). From the car park, go east towards the road entrance that you entered by and take the track that heads towards the hills.
There is a signpost: 'Castlelaw by the Howden Glen, with the co-operation of the landowner'.

Wooded areas contrast sharply with open hill and moorland. This is a walk of variety, through a mosaic of habitats, with the opportunity to enjoy good views in fine weather.

Follow this track, which is tarmac in places, passing a copse of trees on a knoll called Chucklie (mistakenly) or **Chuckie** (correctly) **Knowe**. (The 1852 OS map shows a quarry here, and 'chuckie' is the Scots word for pebble.)

The **place names** in this area are interesting. Dreghorn is recorded as 'Dregerne' in 1240, 'Dregarne' in 1374 and 'Dragorn' in 1682. The name is British, from *dre*, 'the farm', and *gronn*, 'a bog'. Capelaw Hill is part Celtic, *ceap* meaning 'pointed hill' (also referring to the Kips) and part Anglian, *law* also meaning 'conical hill'. The 1794 Statistical Account applies the name Capelaw to Allermuir Hill. For a full description of place names refer to S Harris's *The Place Names of Edinburgh, Their Origins and History* (see bibliography).

Keep on the track, crossing a broken gate, fording a small burn and heading on the track up a grassy area until you eventually cross a bridge and reach a small stone building, **Green Craig Cistern**.

'Edinburgh Thomas Elder Praefect MDCCIXC' is carved on the lintel of **Green Craig Cistern**. Thomas Elder of Forneth was lord provost of Edinburgh from 1788 to 1790, and the construction of a water pipeline to supply the city was begun during his tenure.

Green Craig Cistern, with Arthur's Seat in the distance

Go past the cistern and head up a grassy track to the southwest. Much of the gorse has been cleared to allow native trees and shrubs to be planted, and to encourage natural regeneration.

2 Remain on the track as it climbs up the slope of **White Hill** (not named on OS66) and keep to it on rising ground that can be boggy in places.

3 As the ground levels out you will reach a tumbled-down drystane dyke and you may need to pick your way through the rushes alongside the dyke and fence. Keep on this path until you reach a cattle-grid and gate at NT217665.

Pick up a path that goes right, to the plantation around **Bonaly Reservoir**. Follow the fence and drystane dyke on your right until you reach a gate. Go through the gate and walk straight ahead downhill for a few metres, where there is a signpost indicating Bonaly.

4 Follow the path to Bonaly and you will see Bonaly Reservoir on the left. A pleasant diversion is to walk around the perimeter of the reservoir, picking out a narrow path that starts by the plantation (this is included in the 7km distance for this walk).

The present **Bonaly Reservoir** was constructed in 1851 to replace two smaller reservoirs, built in 1789 when Edinburgh's expanding New Town was placing greater demands on the water supply. In 1786 the town council drew up plans to create two ponds at Bonaly, and after a prolonged court case these reservoirs were built. The abandoned dam at NT212663, to the northeast of the present dam, is a relic of the first reservoir. The present-day reservoir was constructed on the site of the second reservoir.

Back at the point from which you made your diversion round the reservoir, there is a good track leading downhill towards the woodlands of lower **Bonaly Country Park**.

An area of **heather moorland** lies to the west of the track, and curlew, skylark, meadow pipit and red grouse are heard and sometimes seen here. The **views** across to the Ochils and beyond are spectacular on a clear day. To the east, **Dean Burn** cuts its way down a steep rocky gorge. The ungrazed slopes are where juniper, rowan and birch grow, and common blue butterflies feed in sunny spots in summer.

Go through the gate at the top of the woodland, where there is another signpost indicating Bonaly. Follow this track down, past a disused building on the right and a circular stone viewpoint on the left, to reach a car park. Don't go through the gate into the car park.

A sign by the gate at the car park indicates **Dreghorn**. Follow this sign and take a small path that cuts down through the trees to cross a burn by a wooden bridge. The path is very narrow here, and after about 10m ascends to a few steps to the left. An orienteering control post is here in the shrubs.

5 From the top of the steps take this path as it leads off to the east and follows the perimeter fence of **Bonaly Scout Camp**. The path climbs steeply and eventually flattens out, then descends through a grassy area to a gate. There is another signpost indicating Dreghorn just next to the gate. Go through the gate and walk across the field ahead of you, on a grassy path under a line of electricity pylons that marches parallel to the city bypass, roaring 400m away to your left.

Having crossed the field, the path leads onto another track next to a hedge. Stay on this until you reach a cattle-grid, and **Dreghorn Mains**, a ruined farm, is on your left. The farm is about 1km from the gate and previous sign to Dreghorn. A SRWS sign at the cattle-grid points your return to Dreghorn car park, passing the farm buildings and going through a small wooden gate, with the traffic on the bypass tearing by.

Dean Burn Gorge

WALK 4
Three Reservoirs

Distance	9km
Ascent	214m
Time	2 hours and 30 minutes
Maps	Ordnance Survey Landranger 66 or
	Ordnance Survey Explorer 344
Start/Finish	Bonaly car park NT211675

A hill walk taking in three reservoirs. The going is generally easy, and there is a good mix of cultural heritage and wildlife to enjoy along the way. (It is possible to lengthen this route by walking to Harlaw and completing a circuit of the reservoir (Walk 6).)

1 Start at **Bonaly** car park, beyond the scout camp on Bonaly Road.

Note Alternative parking is available just beyond the bridge over the A720, and this is preferable in winter, when the narrow road can be icy and it is difficult to manoeuvre a vehicle. The route from the alternative parking passes **Bonaly Tower**, an integral part of the cultural heritage of the area.

Bonaly Tower was built for Lord Henry Cockburn in 1811. Cockburn was an outstanding lawyer, becoming solicitor-general in 1830 and a judge of the Court of Session in 1834. He was a popular and influential figure, well connected with the great and the good of the day. He founded the Friday Club with Sir Walter Scott in 1803, and often invited friends to spend a hill day at Bonaly. Amongst this circle were James Naysmith, the inventor of the steam hammer, and the artists David Octavius Hill and James Ballantyne. Bonaly Tower is a private residence, now divided into flats. Edinburgh Corporation purchased 65 acres of ground here for the city's water supply, and thus formed the basis of Bonaly Country Park.

From the upper car park (NT211675) go through the gate and take the track that climbs steeply uphill into the plantations, following the signpost that indicates Glencorse until you reach a gate. Go through this gate, which opens out onto heather moorland, and keep on this track, going through yet another gate leading into **Bonaly Reservoir** compound. This is a distance of about 1km.

2 A few metres to the right, take a narrow path in the heather leading over to the north end of Bonaly Reservoir dam. Either walk along the top of the dam, or around the reservoir and then cross the spillway with care. From the spillway go right and then through a gate in the gap in the trees. Here there is a signpost indicating Glencorse. Turn right here and follow a muddy path along the edge of the trees by a fence and dyke.

The prevailing westerly winds are often quite strong at **Bonaly Reservoir**, and it is fairly unsheltered, despite the encircling trees, but it is home to mallard ducks, redshanks and goldeneye, as well as common blue damselflies and common frogs.

3 Keep on this path as it starts to climb **Harbour Hill** – the ground can be boggy in places, especially near the flattish summit.

The name '**Harbour**' is probably from the Anglian *heorde-beorg*, which means 'hill of' (or 'for') 'flocks or herds', i.e. a grazing where stock could be gathered before being shorn or driven to market (see S Harris, bibliography).

In 1910 George Reith commented wryly of the **view** from here, 'We try not to see the ugly chimneys and black smoke of the shale districts; we try also not to smell the latter: unsuccessfully, if the wind be in the north west.' Things have definitely improved since his time – the views on a clear day are good.

4 Keep on the path to walk over Harbour Hill and descend to the good track at the bottom (NT213643),

Maiden's Cleugh – close up of stone stile

and turn right. **Maiden's Cleuch** is the valley between Harbour Hill and Bell's Hill. It crosses the col with a stone stile and a gate close to its crest. Down to the left is **Glencorse Reservoir**, and to the right, **Harlaw** and the north side of the hills. (It is possible to lengthen this route by walking north to Harlaw and completing a circuit of the reservoir (see Route 6).)

Maiden's Cleuch is, according to S Harris (see bibliography), a 20th-century misnomer of what early maps, e.g. Roy 1753, call 'Clochmead' or 'Clochmaid Gate'. The name appears to refer to the gate or track itself, rather than the col it crosses, which is hardly a cleuch or ravine, like Green Cleuch or Dens Cleuch. It is likely a corruption of the Celtic *cloch* or *clach*, meaning 'a stone'. The stone is the huge boulder that forms the boundary and stile at the summit. But the name could also be Gaelic: *cloch meid*, 'the stone at the middle of the pass'.

5 From the gate on the col, take the path to the right towards Harlaw and continue until you reach a gate at **Cock Rig** (marked on OS 344). Go through the gate and take the path, signposted to Currie, that follows the line of the drystane dyke to your right. You will reach another gate at the top of a conifer plantation. ▸

On the other side of the dyke are the remains of brick and stone buildings, now used as sheep pens, and possibly connected to the disused rifle ranges in this area.

6 From the gate at the top of the conifer plantation take a rough and stony track (locally called Ranges Road, but not named on the map) for approximately 1.5km to a white house (once a smiddy) on your right at the end of the road.

This area used to be good for finding odds and ends such as Victorian bottles and earthenware pots, probably from the coup or midden of the smiddy and farm. These artefacts were revealed when some trees were felled, and the soil beneath was lifted to uncover the old crockery.

At the white house turn right. There is a SRWS sign next to the house – take the road marked Torphin and Bonaly. Follow the road past **Mid Kinleith** and a path to the Poet's Glen on your left.

The poet of **Poet's Glen** was James Thomson, known as the Weaver Poet. His cottage, which he named Parnassus, is a little way down the glen, and a private residence. Thomson was brought up by his grandparents in Currie and apprenticed as a weaver to his grandfather. He began to write a few verses, and they gained in popularity and enjoyed wide circulation – at the time Thomson was called the second Burns.

After about 100m go over the stone bridge, where the road becomes a rough track at **East Kinleith farm**.

7 At **East Kinleith** farm the track opens into the farmyard. There are some cottages on your right and a SRWS sign-post opposite them. Follow the SRWS sign indicating Bonaly along a track that passes the end cottage on the right. The track leads through to **Clubbiedean Reservoir**.

Clubbiedean and **Torduff reservoirs** were constructed in 1849 and 1848 to gather water from the North Pentlands Aqueduct to supply Edinburgh. At the western end of Clubbiedean Reservoir there is a small, roughcast building at a corner in the track (NT197667). In the field adjacent to the building, look over the gate straight ahead to see some earth ramparts by the trees – this is Clubbiedean Fort, an Iron Age settlement and Scheduled Ancient Monument. It is not as spectacular or well known as Castlelaw (Walks 5 and 22), and the fort only consists of two concentric earthen ramparts and ditches. Little else was discovered during excavation, and the drystane dykes and trees obliterate the original contents.

The name Clubbiedean is probably from the Scots *clabby*, meaning 'miry', and *dene*, 'a long, winding

Clubbiedean Fort, an Iron Age settlement

valley'. Clubbiedean is a good place to see a variety of waterbirds, such as grey heron, goldeneye, cormorant, mute swan, dabchick and tufted duck. There is a rich variety of water plants, too, making the reservoir a listed wildlife site.

8 Continue on the track, which eventually becomes a metalled road, and follow the signpost indicating Bonaly car park.

9 ▸ The view as you walk down the road reveals Edinburgh at its best, with good vistas of Arthur's Seat and the castle. When you reach the former water-keeper's house, go right across the top of Torduff dam, between two fences, and enter Bonaly Country Park, signposted to Dreghorn.
　　Climb a few steps, then take a narrow path to the left that contours round **Torduff Hill** and enjoy more panoramas over Edinburgh. Stay on this path to head downhill to the gate and then to the car park.

The reservoir in the steep-sided ravine is **Torduff Reservoir**, with scrubby juniper bushes growing on the rocky outcrops above the water.

Armstrong's map of 1773 names **Torduff Hill** 'Torbrack'. Both Torduff and Torbrack are Gaelic and/or British, *torr* meaning 'steep sided', and *dubh* meaning 'black', or *breac* meaning 'speckled', in contrast to the paler and smoother neighbour Torphin.

41

WALK 5
A Phantom Walk

Distance	9km
Ascent	454m
Time	3hours and 30 minutes
Maps	Ordnance Survey Landranger 66
	Ordnance Survey Explorer 344
Start/Finish	Bonaly NT211675

A route with good views from a number of different vantage points, and some fascinating cultural heritage. (This walk could also be started from Castlelaw car park.)

1 The walk begins at **Bonaly** car park (NT211675) just beyond the scout camp.

Note Alternative parking is available just beyond the bridge over the A720, and this is preferable in winter, when the narrow road can be icy and it is difficult to manoeuvre a vehicle.

The name **Bonaly** is recorded from 1280, and early spellings, e.g. 'Bonalyn', show the name as British *banathelan*, 'place of the broom bushes'. The lands here were part of the Redhall estate until 1772, when a local landowner, James Gillespie of Spylaw, joined Bonaly with the western part of his estate, then called Fernielaw. Lord Cockburn then feued (leased) 20 acres and went on to build Bonaly Tower, in the process destroying the village of Bonaly, which was at the confluence of Lady and Dean burns (see also Walk 4).

If it is early morning or late in the day you may catch a glimpse of roe deer, or hear a great spotted woodpecker drumming in spring.

From the car park go through the gate on a track leading to the hill, signposted Glencorse, and ascend the track through the plantations. ◄ The track comes out of the woodland, where there is another signpost indicating Glencorse, and then onto open heather moorland, where there are often meadow pipits and curlews. The spring song and display flight of the curlew (colloquially called a 'whaup') must be one of the most evocative sounds in the hills.

Continue on the track for a further kilometre until you reach the trees surrounding **Bonaly Reservoir**. If you have time, detour round the reservoir (see Walks 3 and 4). Leave the fenced reservoir compound by the gate at the eastern side, where there is a signpost indicating Glencorse, and take the path that skirts the western side of **Capelaw Hill**. ▶

Despite its Celtic meaning – 'pointed hill' – Capelaw is far from pointed; rather, it is a big, whale-backed lump of a place.

2 The path curves round and down **Phantom's Cleuch**, crossing a small wooden bridge at NT211652.

Army signage in the Phantom's Cleugh

Phantom's Cleuch is so-named after a mysterious character nicknamed 'the Phantom' by the Ranger Service. This individual was seen about the hills carrying a spade and doing minor path repairs, or clearing water bars and cross drains. Whenever a ranger tried to approach the man to thank him for his efforts, he walked away and could not be engaged in conversation. He has not been seen in the hills for some ten years now, and as he was not young, he may have passed away or become too infirm to continue his sterling work. When the Ranger Service was approached by Harveys Maps to amend its Pentland Hills Superwalker map, we added the name Phantom's Cleuch to mark his efforts.

The path heads downhill over the grassy ground of **Knightfield Rig**, past ruined **Kirkton Cottage** to join the Maiden's Cleuch path from **Harlaw** to your right. ◄

During the 1930s, and perhaps before, the inhabitants of Kirkton Cottage served tea and scones to parties of walkers. Many people still remember the food and drink supplied from the cottage.

3 Go down to the gate at the bottom of the Maiden's Cleuch path and out onto the glen road by Glencorse Reservoir. The signpost here indicates Flotterstone. Turn left and walk down the road, crossing Kirk Bridge, and continue on for about 400m until you reach a gate by a pine plantation on your left.

At the signpost here, follow the finger that points to **Castlelaw**, through the gate and up a stony path between a tumbled-down drystane dyke and trees. ▶ Turn right at the top gate and take the track signposted to Castlelaw.

(**Note** The land to the north of the track is used for military training, and there are two firing ranges. For your own safety, please keep well clear of the danger area by staying on the track. Even when live firing is taking place, access around Castlelaw and the earth house is unrestricted.)

Staying on the track, go through three kissing gates, and follow the sign, adjacent to the Ranges Building, indicating Castlelaw.

4 Walk around the perimeter of **Castlelaw** farm steading, and at a small car park (NT229637) by sheep pens, go uphill and through another a kissing gate to the hill fort, with a signpost next to it reading 'Dreghorn 3M'.

Castlelaw hill fort is in the care of Historic Scotland, and interpretation boards have been provided. The ramparts and ditches are quite clear, especially so in low winter sunlight, which accentuates the shadows. The Iron Age people living here would have built a wooden palisade, and within this were timber round-houses and space to keep livestock. Also at the site is a souterrain, for cool storage of grain, meat and cheese, which was used after the camp was abandoned. Evidence of Roman pottery and animal bones was found when the earth house was excavated in 1932 by Professor Gordon Childe. (There are four ancient camps on the southeastern hills: Hillend, Castlelaw, Lawhead and Camp Hill (Braidwood).)

There is a good variety of fungi found here in the autumn. I've found very good specimens of 'the blusher' (*Amanita rubescens*).

Castlelaw hill fort

W Anderson (see bibliography) rated the views from here as the best in the whole of the Pentlands, especially good for winter sunsets.

Leave the hill fort and walk up the stony track towards the east side of **Castlelaw Hill**. The track climbs gradually, and the view over the Midlothian plain opens out. After about 500m there is a rough path leading to the summit of Castlelaw Hill. If it is a clear day, make the short ascent to the top of the hill. ◄

5 Return from Castlelaw Hill to the main track and continue over good ground to **Fala Knowe** (shown on OS 344) at NT226655. The name Fala Knowe derives from the Scots *faw law*, meaning 'speckled' hill of a 'conical' or 'cairn-like' shape. From Fala Knowe the view back along the backbone ridge of the Pentlands is superb, and even better with a light dusting of snow.

Continue over Fala Knowe on the track as it descends to a cattle-grid. Cross the cattle-grid and after 300m reach a point where another path crosses the main track. Take this path to the left, down through the heather, over a stile, and then along a narrow but good path that contours around the north side of **Capelaw Hill**.

Once the lower part of **Bonaly Country Park** is reached, a short diversion is to wander down through the woodland on either side of the track.

6 The path drops downhill, back towards Bonaly Reservoir, surrounded by trees. Go through the gate, past the reservoir on your left, and back down the track towards the start. ◄

The woodland area to the west of the track is known by the Ranger Service as Sanctuary Wood, and **Blacklaws Burn** flows down through the trees. It is named on a 1799 map as 'Blackmyre Syke', or 'small burn', but the name Blacklaws is used on the 1852 Ordnance Survey map. Blacklaws may derive from 'Blacklache', from the Anglian *laecc*, 'boggy stream', with 'black' referring to its course through peaty moorland.

Enjoy good views over to Fife and beyond in clear weather on the descent back to the car park at Bonaly.

WALK 6
Harlaw Reservoir Circuit

Distance	3km
Ascent	Flat
Time	45 minutes
Maps	Ordnance Survey Landranger 66 or
	Ordnance Survey Explorer 344
Start/Finish	Harlaw car park NT181654

1 Start at Harlaw car park, just off Harlaw Road, reached by going past some cottages at **Harlaw Farm**. The car park is located in some trees, hidden from the road. (If the car park is full, park on one side of the road only. Please use the grass verge by the hedge leading up from the farm, and park well onto the verge to allow wide farm machinery to access the fields.)

At the car park there is an SRWS sign indicating 'Harlaw, Threipmuir & Glencorse'. Take either the path leading through woodland towards **Harlaw House**, or turn right at the field gates and reach it by walking along the road by the hedge.

This hedge is a good place to catch glimpses of **wildlife**. Look out for bullfinches, accompanied by their rather depressing call note, and the more cheery chaffinch and greenfinch, which are also frequent visitors. Stoats

A pleasant woodland stroll beside Harlaw Reservoir, this is not a hill walk, more an excellent short circular walk when the weather on the tops is wild, or you're short of time and want a quick stretch of the legs. The wildlife interest is also good. (Walk 6 is easy to extend by joining either Walk 7 or Walk 8 at the stone stile leading to Black Springs.)

Harlaw wildlife garden – great for a picnic or for wildlife-friendly gardening tips

are sometimes seen here, usually whizzing across the road in search of rabbits, wood mice or short-tailed voles.

Pay a visit to the **wildlife garden** at Harlaw House – it's a peaceful spot and has something of interest at any time of year. Large interpretation panels have been installed, to let you know what you should be able to see. In spring, if the pond has not dried out, it's a good spot for common frogs spawning – the croaking can be heard from quite a distance away. Palmate newts can also be glimpsed in the pond. The wildflower meadow has developed over the years, with a profusion of black knapweed, red campion, common spotted orchid and ox-eye daisies catching the breeze.

Harlaw House is the former water-keeper's cottage. It was originally single storey, then an extra storey was added to accommodate the water keeper's family. In 1996 it was converted to single storey again, for use as a base for the Pentland Hills Ranger Service. There are a couple of rooms with displays, leaflets and informa-tion about the Pentland Hills Regional Park. The house is open daily (except Christmas Day and New Year's

Day), but please check times as they may vary (telephone the Pentland Hills Ranger Service on 0131 445 3383 or check www.pentlandhills.org for opening times).

From Harlaw House go straight ahead along a path signposted Harlaw Woodland Walk. ▶ The path leads into woodland and winds its way between trees of varying ages and heights, although they are dominated by Scots pines, then crosses a narrow stone bridge and a set of stone steps in a dyke. There is an alternative path to Black Springs here, and both Walks 7 and 8 are good extensions to this walk, otherwise carry on with the main path.

There is a good view towards the bulk of Black Hill and the conical 'volcano pretender' West Kip in the distance.

Black Hill looms moodily, its heathery slopes patterned by muirburn (the deliberate burning of mature heather). Lapwings (known locally as peewits) sometimes nest or feed in the fields on the south side of the dyke. The 17th-century Covenanters disliked the birds, as its call was said to betray the whereabouts of the Covenanters to their pursuers. (The collective noun for peewits is a 'deceit'.) The path side is good for wild flowers – in season there is sneezewort, lady's bedstraw, devil's bit scabious (known locally as 'curlie doddie'), meadowsweet and wood avens. Many of these have been used in herbal medicine for hundreds of years.

2 After about a kilometre go through a field gate in the dyke and a grassy bank faces you. This is **Threipmuir Reservoir dam**, and it's a pleasant stroll along the top (if it's not too blowy). Enjoy the vista over the Threipmuir. ▶

Return to the path and cross the spillway by the metal bridge to the right, through a gap in the dyke. A signpost at the far end of the bridge indicates Harlaw Ranger Centre. In times of heavy rain the flow over the spillway can be quite spectacular. The path to **Harlaw** is straight ahead, although you may wish to divert amongst the trees parallel to the path.

In winter greylag and pink-footed geese roost here, as do gulls and a variety of waterfowl.

In 2003 an unusual **fungus** appeared at the base of one of the pines here. It was a cauliflower fungus (*Sparassis crispa*), and is certainly well named. The woodland around Harlaw is good for fungi, and the deceiver, fly agaric, brown birch bolete, slippery Jack, brown roll rim and cep have all been found here.

3 The path curves around and heads to the spillway across **Harlaw dam** – again a metal bridge has been provided to allow a safe crossing.

There is a dyke along the length of Harlaw dam with a stone stile through it. Often on the stonework of the dyke there is a **mink** scat (dropping), a tarry smudge with telltale fish scales and bones mixed in. Mink scat has an unpleasant odour, unlike otter spraint. The mink makes its mark by leaving a scat at a conspicuous place, warning others of its presence. The reservoir is stocked with trout, which no doubt satisfies the mink.

View over Harlaw Reservoir

Return to Harlaw car park either by the road or via the woodland walk.

WALK 7
*Black Hill, Green Cleuch
and Red Moss*

Distance	8.5km
Ascent	125m
Time	2 hours and 20 minutes
Maps	Ordnance Survey Landranger 66 or
	Ordnance Survey Explorer 344
Start/Finish	Harlaw car park NT181654

1 Begin the walk at **Harlaw** car park (as for Walk 6). Follow the Harlaw Woodland Walk past Harlaw House, and go straight ahead south, towards the woodland around **Harlaw Reservoir**.

This is a quiet circuit, with good views despite its modest height gain. As it includes Black Hill, Green Cleuch and Red Moss, it will probably bring some colour to your cheeks.

View over the quiet waters at Black Springs (PHRS)

Shortly after going over a narrow stone bridge you'll see some stone steps crossing the dyke, and a signpost pointing towards **Black Springs**. Cross the dyke using the stone steps and follow the direction of the signpost, again going straight ahead to a stile. Climb the stile and then ascend a slight rise between some young trees. At the brow of the rise cross two further stiles, and then make downhill on the path towards the eastern arm of **Threipmuir Reservoir**, called Black Springs.

2 Stay on the same path, climb yet another stile and you're at Black Springs.

Black Springs is important for wildlife. It has the second largest area of reedbed in the Lothians (Duddingston Loch at Holyrood Park, Edinburgh, being the largest) and is home to the reed bunting and sedge warbler. You may also be fortunate enough to hear the pig-like squeal of a water rail as it skulks among the reeds. The water rail is especially adapted to this habitat, its body being flattened to allow it to run through the reeds with ease. Its bright-red bill is a multi-tool, used for picking up seeds and insects, snatching small fish, or clubbing nestlings and mice.

The quiet waters here are where mute swans and, in winter, whooper swans are sometimes seen.

From the stile turn right and follow the path through gorse towards a small stone building (NT188641), crossing the dam and another stile to reach the building. ▶

3 Just beyond the building go up an eroded path beside the drystane dyke to your right. Follow the path as it hugs the south side of the dyke on a gradual journey on the lower slopes of **Black Hill**. This path is very peaty and eroded in places, so is probably best avoided after wet weather. From the path there are good views over Threipmuir Reservoir, and to Harlaw and beyond.

Keep on this path for about 1.5km until it descends quite steeply to **Green Cleuch**. Green Cleuch is the narrow valley between Black Hill and Hare Hill (marked on OS 344.)

The stone building is a collecting point for the water gathered from the numerous springs dotted amongst the heather and bracken in this area.

The green and pleasant Beech Avenue

4 Go right here over a stile and take this pleasant route through the valley for about 1.5km, crossing a burn on the way. The path ends at another stile and gate by a wall. Cross the stile and walk down the road, passing the driveway to **Bavelaw Castle** on your right.

5 At the top of a steep hill (where there is a signpost indicating Balerno) turn right down the road, known locally as **Beech Avenue,** and enjoy the descent between beech trees to a stone bridge at NT164630.

This is **Redford Bridge**, and an excellent vantage point from which to view the birds that use **Threipmuir Reservoir**. There is also a bird hide about 200m along on the southern shore. It is accessed by going over a stile and following a narrow path over some wooden sleeper bridges and a boardwalk.

The place name **Redford** may refer to the marshy ground here, hence 'reedy ford', or it may have been named after the reddish colour of the earth or stones on the bed of the burn. **Threipmuir** is recorded in 1812 as 'Threap Muir', the Scots *threpe* meaning 'debatable'. This would seem plausible, as Threipmuir lies at the border between Malleny, Bavelaw and Kirkton estates, and its ownership may have been contentious.

The area to the west of the bridge is called **Bavelaw Marsh** and, along with Red Moss, is a site of special scientific interest (SSSI). The marsh used to be an important habitat for wintering wildfowl, and had a noisy black-headed gull colony, although in recent years both these have declined. The exposed silt and mud in the autumn make a superb feeding ground for waders such as redshank, snipe and green sandpiper. It is also worth checking for rare waders, and birdwatchers come here regularly to scan the marsh.

After leaving Redford Bridge, walk along the road. Continue along the tarmac until you reach a narrow path leading off to the right through a wood. ◄

Partially hidden in the trees to the right is ruined Redford Stables, reputed to have been used by Mary Queen of Scots.

6 Take the narrow path, which goes along the edge of **Redford Birch Wood**, signposted to Harlaw. ▸

Where the path joins the tarmac there is an information board about the fascinating wildlife found in the area.

The Ranger Service manages **Redford Birch Wood**, with the aim of sustaining it as a birch wood. Towards the wood's centre there are signs of the felling that took place in 2004, to allow new seedlings to regenerate with plenty of light.

After 300m the path emerges onto the track near Threipmuir car park. Go right here, where the sign indicates Harlaw again, and on a rough track walk past a plantation to your right and through a gate, leading back to a fishing hut by Threipmuir Reservoir.

7 Take the track alongside the reservoir to the spillway and dam. When you reach the spillway, don't cross it, but keep up to the left on a narrow path through the trees, and then turn left to join the track on the western side of **Harlaw Reservoir**.

8 Cross Harlaw Reservoir spillway and dam and go past Harlaw House to return to the car park via your outward route.

The beauty of a great crested grebe on a carved sign at Bavelaw (PHRS)

WALK 8
Carnethy and Turnhouse

Distance	15km
Ascent	454m
Time	4 hours and 30 minutes
Maps	Ordnance Survey Landranger 66 or
	Ordnance Survey Explorer 344
Start/Finish	Harlaw car park NT181654

This walk starts gently, preparing you for the steeper sections of the route up over Carnethy and Turnhouse Hill, and the wind will usually be at your back over the tops.

1 Begin the walk at **Harlaw** car park, NT181654, leaving through the field gates to head southeast on a track between the fields. The signpost by the field gates indicates Glencorse.

After about 200m the track divides – take the fork off to the right towards a small plantation. At the plantation go through another gate, and then head off to the left on a path signposted to **Black Springs**. This path goes over four stiles as it climbs over a slight rise to dip down to Black Springs.

2 At the fourth stile, go right on the path through gorse and then walk over the dam to the Black Springs hut.

Black Hill in winter (PHRS)

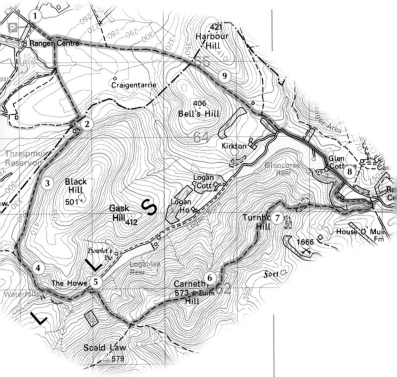

3 Behind the
hut, take a wet, rather peaty path to the right, as it hugs
the drystane dyke along the edge of **Black Hill**. The path
climbs gradually before contouring round and down to
Green Cleuch.

Black Hill and the Pentlands were an inspirational
spark for the Everest climber **Dougal Haston**. In his
2002 book about Haston, *Dougal Haston: The
Philosophy of Risk*, Jeff Connor says, 'The range's modest tops offer extensive views over the Forth Valley to
the Ochil Hills in the north and, on a clear day, round
to Ben Lomond in the west. The Pentlands culminate in

57

Waterfall at the Howe

a highest point at Scald Law (579m), but for Haston these lowly fells stirred a passion that was to guide his life.'

4 At Green Cleuch the path is well made and stony, in contrast to the eroded soil of Black Hill. Head left (southeast) and keep on this path, passing **Logan Burn** waterfall.

The area around **Logan Burn waterfall** is a site of special scientific interest (SSSI), designated in 1985 for its rare, lime-loving plants. Wood sorrel, great wood-rush, opposite-leaved golden saxifrage, yellow pimpernel, rock rose and limestone bedstraw have been recorded here.

5 The waterfall is spectacular in spate, but the path hugs the hillside above the burn, and a wooden footbridge is in place to ensure a safe crossing. The cleuch eventually opens out to a sheep-grazed area, which is regionally important for its fungi.

This grassy area of the cleuch supports at least 16 different species of **waxcap fungi**, and they are worth searching for in autumn for their reds and yellows. With names such as parrot waxcap, scarlet hood and pink ballet dancer, they add an exotic palette to the grass.

The **geology** here is also of interest. The Green Cleuch glacial channel was formed at the end of the ice age. Although most of the ice had begun to melt, remnants of ice from the northwestern edge of the hills burst through the gap between Black Hill and Hare Hill, scouring out Green Cleuch, and then continuing to form Flotterstone Glen as we see it today. Dens Cleuch, between Black Hill and Bell's Hill, was formed later in a similar way. Logan Burn waterfall was cut *after* the Green Cleuch glacial channel.

At the grassy sheep-grazed area, take a path that climbs steeply up to your right, signposted Penicuik and Kirk Road. Ascend this path, climbing a wooden stile on the way up to the bealach between **Scald Law** on the right and **Carnethy Hill** on the left.

6 Keep on the path up Carnethy Hill – at the summit (573m) there is a large tumbled-down cairn.

The name **Carnethy Hill** comes from the early British word *carneddau*, meaning 'hill of the cairns'. The cairn is early Bronze Age and a Scheduled Ancient Monument. Carnethy was much admired by Sir Walter Scott, who on 11 November 1827 wrote in his journal, 'I think, I never saw anything more beautiful than the ridge of Caernethy against a clear, frosty sky, with its peaks and varied slopes. The hills glowed like purple amethyst, the sky glowed topaz and vermillion colours. I never saw a finer screen than Pentland, considering that it is neither rocky nor highly elevated.'

Continue straight ahead (east) on the path as it descends and then climbs from a col to **Turnhouse Hill**.

Dotterel are sometimes seen in passage here – there are at least two records in recent years for this area. Dotterel are odd birds, not only reversing gender roles, but surprisingly approachable and easily trapped – perhaps giving rise to the word 'dotty', and their scientific name, *morinellus*, meaning 'little fool'.

Turnhouse Hill also sports a cairn, although less impressive than its neighbour.

7 ◄ Stay on the path and make the descent off Turnhouse Hill, past some wind-sculpted larches, towards Flotterstone. Cross a couple of stiles before reaching a wooden bridge to your left, over **Glencorse Burn**.

Cross the bridge, go through a gate and turn left onto a rough track, following a signpost marked to the filter beds. Walk along this rough track, going through two self-closing gates and past a neat stone circular building, before coming to an old bothy and the filter beds tucked away in the valley.

> This is a good spot for the **green woodpecker,** although you are more likely to hear its laughing call than to see it. Ian Munro, in *The Birds of the Pentland Hills* (see bibliography), remarks that the green woodpecker was unknown in the hills until after the Second World War. The bird is more often seen feeding on the ground, searching for ants and other insects, which it scoops up with its long tongue. Sometimes its droppings can be found, which look like cigarette ash.

8 Walk on and up the track to a white gate, and a self-closing gate leading out onto Flotterstone Glen road at NT224634. Turn left and walk up the road past picturesque **Glen Cottage**, the former water-keeper's house, with **Glencorse Reservoir** unfolding gradually to your left.

> **Glencorse Reservoir** has a pine-covered island, which may have a causeway, depending on the water level. This area has a Highland feel to it, partly due to the patchwork of water, hills and pines. Film companies like this location for this reason, and probably because the weather is kinder and distances shorter.

Continue along the road (ignoring the signpost to Castlelaw by the plantation), walking on over **Kirk Bridge**, until you come to a gate and a self-closing gate on your right by another plantation.

9 There is a signpost here – follow the finger indicating Balerno by Harlaw, and take the track uphill. The track climbs gradually, ascending 110m over 1.5km, up to the stile and gates at the apex of Maiden's Cleuch. Continue straight ahead for a fairly easy descent north back to Harlaw car park.

WALK 9
Three Peaks

Distance	13km
Ascent	484m
Time	4 hours
Maps	Ordnance Survey Landranger 66 or
	Ordnance Survey Explorer 344
Start/Finish	Threipmuir car park NT166638

A fine walk with a gradual build up. This route can be enjoyed and varied according to the weather and one's mood.

1 This walk begins from **Threipmuir** car park NT166638. The car park is a good place to listen and look for small woodland birds. Willow warbler and chiffchaff are abundant in summer, with bullfinch, robin and wren in winter. Leave the car park at the western side and head left along the road towards **Red Moss** nature reserve. A signpost located at the junction of the road and the car park indicates Nine Mile Burn 4M and Glencorse 5M.

If you have time, divert for a short walk along the **Red Moss's** boardwalk, which takes you round the sensitive habitats of the area without causing damage. Red Moss and Bavelaw Marsh together form **Balerno Common**, a site of special scientific interest (SSSI) designated in 1986. Red Moss is a lowland raised peat bog with areas of woodland, and contains many rare and interesting plants, such as bog asphodel, cranberry, round-leaved sundew and lesser twayblade, as well as five species of sphagnum moss. The reserve is managed by the Scottish Wildlife Trust, and has interpretation boards to explain the formation of the bog and the plants found there.

Continue up the road across **Redford Bridge** and up **Beech Avenue**. At the top of the hill turn right, following the signpost for Nine Mile Burn. After about 60m turn left at another signpost, also indicating Nine Mile Burn, and then reach a field gate and a self-closing gate.

Go through the gate, then head straight ahead on the track known locally as the Red Road (because of the red soil that is evident on part of the path, although this name is not marked on any map), alongside a plantation of conifers.

2 After about 750m on the Red Road you may wish to divert across the northwest side of **Hare Hill** to a plaque just below the summit.

Just below the summit of **Hare Hill** there is a small wooden post and plaque in the rushes and heather (the post is located at NT171621). These mark the site where a German Junkers 88 bomber, hit by anti-aircraft fire over Pilton, north of Edinburgh, in March 1943, lost height and exploded when it hit the ground. The pilot, Fritz Forster, and his three crew were killed. The RAF

Hare Hill crash site

removed the wreckage and the airmen were buried at Kirknewton. The plaque was unveiled in August 1999 in a ceremony attended by Fritz Forster's son, daughter and grand-daughter. There are still pieces of metal and twisted wreckage lying around.

Hare Hill is shown on Roy's map of 1753. It is generally lighter than neighbouring Black Hill, and its name could therefore be from the Anglian *har hyll*, meaning 'grey hill'.

Back on the track, continue for about 1.5km to a gate in a drystane dyke. The gate is known as the **Red Gate**, and although this name is not shown on any map, it is probably so called because of the red-coloured soil on the track.

The next part of the route can be walked either clockwise as described here, or anti-clockwise – by climbing West Kip, East Kip and then Scald Law, and returning through Green Cleuch and back along the path on the south side of Hare Hill. (Anti-clockwise may be preferable if the prevailing westerly wind is strong or gusty.)

This path continues for 2km before plunging down into **Green Cleuch**. This path is known by the Ranger Service as the Sweep Road, although the origin of the name is unclear.

Go through the Red Gate, and after approximately 20m locate a path to your left, just after a depression in the ground and close to a wooden waymarker (an excellent place to stop for refreshments, sheltered from the wind), and walk along here. The path is peaty and wet in places, but rewarded by the unfolding view of the Kips and Scald Law. ◄

3 As the path reaches Green Cleuch, turn right and go through the valley past Logan Burn waterfall. Follow the stony and grassy track towards the house at **The Howe**, before which there is a sign for a footpath to Penicuik and Kirk Road.

4 Ascend steeply up the signposted footpath, crossing a stile and then following a stony track to the bealach between **Carnethy Hill** and **Scald Law**. At the bealach turn right and take the track as it snakes to the top of Scald Law, at 579m the highest point of the Pentland Hill range.

5 An Ordnance Survey triangulation pillar marks the summit of Scald Law. Enjoy the views all around, then press on straight ahead, first to **East Kip** and then **West Kip**.

6 There are no route-finding difficulties here. Follow the path on the ridge as it roller-coasters along to West Kip.

7 West Kip looks quite pointed and difficult to climb, particularly from Harlaw, but it is actually quite straightforward. Take care on the steep, grassy descent of the hill, though, as it can be slippery. At the base of the hill the signpost points to Balerno.

8 At the signpost follow the finger pointing to Balerno (north), on a pleasant track that crosses **Logan Burn** on a well-constructed stone bridge, then joins another track back at the Red Gate.

From the Red Gate the return journey retraces your outward steps along the Red Road, then Beech Avenue, Redford Bridge and Red Moss, before returning to the start point at Threipmuir car park.

Trig pillar on Scald Law

WALK 10
Pentland Classic

Distance	17km
Ascent	457m
Time	5 hours
Maps	Ordnance Survey Landranger 66 or
	Ordnance Survey Explorer 344
Start/Finish	Threipmuir car park NT166638

I have described this as a classic walk because it contains all the essential ingredients of a good hill day: hills with different characters, a lovely ridge, superb views, great in all seasons, and plenty of natural and cultural heritage interest. It also has the advantage of offering an option to stop for refreshment about halfway through (at Flotterstone), and walking with your back to the prevailing wind.

1 Begin the walk at **Threipmuir** car park (NT166638). Leave the car park at the western side (there is a signpost indicating Nine Mile Burn 4M and Glencorse 5M at the junction of the road and the car park) and head along the road towards **Redford Bridge**. Cross the bridge and walk up the road, lined by beech trees (known locally as Beech Avenue, although not named as such on maps).

At the top of the avenue of beeches turn right (again signposted for Nine Mile Burn), and then after 60m turn left on a rough track and go through a self-closing gate (next to a

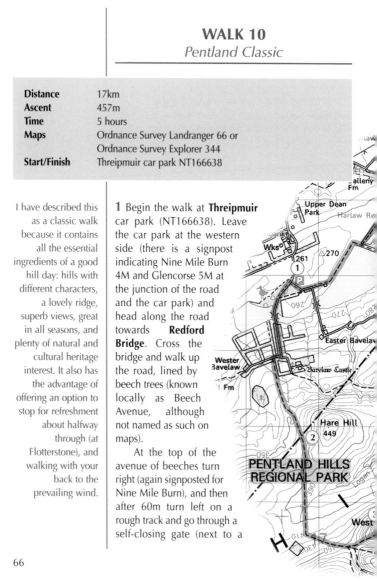

field gate). The path on the other side of the gate is known as the Red Road.

To the west of the Red Road and beyond is the extensive grouse moorland of **Hare Hill**. This patchwork of heather is maintained for the benefit of red grouse, but is also favoured by many other birds, mammals and insects. The red grouse is the iconic game bird of the hills. Its sudden volatile appearance, accompanied by a staccato 'go back, go back, go back' call, is an experience every walker will associate with heather moors. The piles of white grit along the path are to aid the birds' digestion of heather shoots, and to administer a medicine to combat a threadworm that parasitises the birds.

2 Go along the Red Road, initially alongside a conifer plantation, then through another gate by some sheep fanks (pens), and gradually ascend to the crest of the path, before going through a gate. There is a signpost here indicating Nine Mile Burn 2.5M. Keep on this track, crossing a well-constructed stone bridge over **Logan Burn** before climbing again to the foot of **West Kip**.

3 The path here is well worn and quite stepped. Ascend West Kip by the stepped, grassy slope and enjoy the ridge.

4 Continue straight ahead on the path along the ridge in the direction of **East Kip**. There is a small dip before the path rises again over East Kip, then descend again, and at **Cross Sward** (marked on OS 344) go right on a path.

5 Cross peaty ground on this path, and if you want to visit **South Black Hill**, a short climb brings you to the summit cairn.

6 Return to the path and follow it as it veers to the right the top of **Scald Law**, marked by an Ordnance Survey trig pillar at 579m. Drink in the air and the views. From the summit the descent requires care, as the path has many loose stones. It zigzags down to the bealach at the **Old Kirk Road**.

The people of Logan valley would walk over this **Old Kirk Road pass** to church in Penicuik every Sabbath, and coffins would be borne over the same route – quite a last journey. Ten kilometres, with an ascent and descent of 670m, is a good walk every week. The parish of Penicuik swelled in numbers when the populations of Bavelaw and Logan valley were added. When a census was conducted, the surveyor was granted the use of a pony to enable him to travel throughout the parish.

7 From the bealach cross the stile and go straight ahead on the wide path to make the easy ascent of **Carnethy Hill**, with its large summit cairn.

8 Continue straight ahead on the path from the cairn, and descend again to a shallow dip before climbing to the cairn on **Turnhouse Hill**. From Turnhouse Hill walk down the well-worn path, past wind-sculpted trees, and cross two stiles. The slopes fall away sharply down to the valley of **Glencorse Burn**, and two grassy knolls with bracken-cloaked sides signal the end of the ridge.

Scald Law and East and West Kip

At the foot of the last knoll there is a wooden foot-bridge to your left. Cross this bridge (over Glencorse Burn) and here you have a choice. You can either go right to **Flotterstone**, where there are facilities and refreshments at the Flotterstone Inn (500m), or continue left along the main route of the walk.

The main route is along the track leading to some old filter beds (as signposted). It goes through two self-closing gates and passes a circular stone building and a stone bothy by the three former filter beds. Walk past the filter beds and take the track uphill, leading to a white wooden gate with a small self-closing gate next to it.

Go through the gate and turn left onto **Flotterstone Glen** road. Walk by lovely **Glen Cottage**, once the water-keeper's house, and along the road for approximately 1km until you reach a gate on the right, just after crossing **Kirk Bridge** at a bend in the road.

9 Go through the gate and along the path, signposted to Balerno by Harlaw, through **Maiden's Cleuch**. Keep on this path as it climbs up to the bealach between **Bell's**

Maiden's Cleugh sign

West Kip from Harlaw

Hill and **Harbour Hill**. Follow the well-made path to the shelter belt and car park at **Harlaw**. ▶

The name Bell's Hill is first recorded on Knox's map of 1812. It may be early Scots *bellit* hill, meaning 'hill with a bald or bare patch' or possibly Old Norse *bjalli*, meaning 'bell-shaped or rounded hill'.

10 From the car park take the metalled road leading to the left, signposted Harlaw, and walk along to **Harlaw House**. ▶

To complete the walk, take the track that goes across the top of **Harlaw Reservoir** dam, then over the spillway and onto the track before skirting the trees to the north of the reservoir. After 500m or so you will reach **Threipmuir Reservoir** spillway. A signpost here indicates Threipmuir car park. Go in this direction, keeping to the track that goes along the north shore and past a fishing hut.

Go through two gates as the track climbs gently, passing a track to your left. Remain on the track, and in the trees ahead, to your right, return to your starting point.

Harlaw House and its wildlife garden are a good place for a well-earned breather. The garden offers a grand view of West Kip, which you probably left about three hours ago.

WALK 11
Thieves' Road

Distance	27km
Ascent	484m
Time	7 hours 30 minutes
Maps	Ordnance Survey Landranger 65 or Ordnance Survey Explorer 344
Start/Finish	Little Vantage car park NT101628

This is a full day's walk, and gives a real flavour of the Pentlands away from the crowds. Part of this walk is on the infamous Thieves' Road, used by Border reivers driving their stolen cattle. This wild and lonely part of the hills is rich in history.

1 The walk begins at **Little Vantage** car park (NT101628) on the A70 Lanark road (known locally as the Lang Whang).

Next to the car park are the ruins of the **Little Vantage tollhouse**, one of a series of tollhouses located along the road to Lanark. Will Grant, in *The Call of the Pentlands*, says 'In the beginning of the last [19th] century three coaches a week started from the Grassmarket and Princes Street for Lanark by the Lang Whang; and Currie Inn, 'Jenny's Toll' (nine miles from Edinburgh), 'Boll of Bere', 'House on the Muir', 'Little Vantage', 'Cairns Castle Inn', 'Half-way House' – halfway between Edinburgh and Lanark, situated between Wester Causey-end and

Little Vantage stell (PHRS)

Crosswood Burn – and 'South Toun Toll-bar' (Tarbrax), where the first change of horses was made, were all places of bustle and good cheer.'

Leave the car park at the gate by the interpretation panel and head south on a path alongside the dyke, crossing footbridges at **Gala Ford** and skirting round **Harperrig** farm (the ground can be very wet and boggy in places).

2 Gradually you leave flatter ground and start to ascend on the path to the **Cauldstane Slap**, the pass between **East** and **West Cairn Hills**.

The Cauldstane Slap is steeped in history (which can be fully explored by reading the books by W Grant and R Cochrane – see bibliography). The Covenanters met here for their secret gatherings, or conventicles, in the 17th century. One such meeting, on Sunday 8 June 1684, records 200 or 300 men and women, the former armed with blunderbusses, swords and pistols, at the Cauldstane Slap. General Dalyell had been called upon to discover and apprehend those present. The Killing Times had been felt since the thwarted Pentland Rising in 1666, and continued through to the Battle of Drumclog in 1689 and beyond – bloody times indeed.

The walk follows the Old Drove Road, once called the Thieves' Road. Centuries ago this was a lawless and dangerous place, and one that merited the building of a castle stronghold at **Cairns** (NT091605). The castle has an interesting history and once belonged to Sir George Crichton, High Admiral of Scotland. The town of Cairns in northern Australia takes its name from here.

3 We leave the Old Drove road here, and at the fence on the Cauldstane Slap go left (east) up **East Cairn Hill**. There is a path over peaty ground that ascends the hill and veers off to the large cairn at 561m. The view on a clear day is stunning.

The cairn on **East Cairn Hill** is a scheduled ancient monument. Will Grant, in *The Call of the Pentlands*, says, 'The hill now known as the East Cairn Hill gets its present name from the druidical Cairn on the summit, said by some to be a Bronze Age Cairn, probably some 4000 years old, and its ancient name, Harper Hill, from the Bards who used the harp as an accompaniment to their songs. Hence there is the double significance in the two names, in all that the Cairn stands for, and in connection with the ancient harper. The Bards were of the Order of the Druids, and the Druids were often likewise Bards.' Pete Drummond of the Scottish Place Name Society disputes Grant's romantic explanation, saying 'I think the truth is more prosaic – that it was simply named after the farm, Harperrig, at the foot.'

Grant is definitely incorrect when he says that the cairn is at the summit. The true summit is 500m to the east, at NT129595, and 567m on OS 344.

'Spyoncop' carved on a stone

From the cairn follow the dyke on your right and a rough and boggy path eastwards.

In the dyke there is what looks like the word '**spyoncop**' scratched onto a large stone. 'Spionkop' (or 'Spioenkop', from the Afrikaans for 'spy hill') was a battle fought on 23 January 1900 during the Second Boer War. The battle resulted in a British retreat and the loss of 300 men. Surviving British soldiers from Lancashire named their local football stands 'the Kop', the most famous being at Liverpool's Anfield stadium. The Scottish Rifles (or Cameronians, named after Richard Cameron, a notable Covenanter) fought at Spionkop, and the word may have been etched by a surviving soldier, as this area was near where the regiment recruited.

4 After a further kilometre you reach the **Bore Stane** – or Boar Stane – and wind-sculpted larches and Scots pines. Whether wild boar did forage here is a matter for speculation. Go through a gate to your right and follow the signpost 'Carlops 3M' to head south on a path towards **North Esk Reservoir**.

North Esk Reservoir was constructed in 1848 to supply water power to the paper mills of Penicuik. The reservoir is now a nature reserve and home to a noisy colony of black-headed gulls. There is a replica shooting butt that contains an information panel about the wildlife found here.

In the 1880s, when the water level was particularly low, several long cists (burial chambers) containing human remains were uncovered on one of the islands. In 1905, when the site was re-examined, nine cists were found, and what may have been the positions of three others identified. They are part of a small cemetery site. The remains were believed to be early Christian in origin, because the bodies were laid out to their full length, rather than in the foetal position that was more characteristic of burials from earlier times.

5 Follow the path at the west side of North Esk Reservoir down past the cottage (again signposted to Carlops), and then down a rough track for approximately 2km past the house at **Fairliehope** to **Carlops**.

6 The busy A702(T) runs through Carlops, so stay beside the road, going right (west) until you reach a track that leads to the Pentland Icelandic Trekking Centre. (There is also a SRWS signpost that indicates a public path to West Linton.) From the trekking centre continue to follow the track.

The track passes a series of interesting landforms – knolls and hummocks with names such as **Seven Cauldrons**, **Hollow Haugh** and **Hell's Hole** (further descriptions of this area are given in Walk 16). These

North Esk Reservoir

knolls and hummocks are the remains of glacial activity from about 10,000 years ago.

Keep on the track, which follows the course of a Roman road, until you reach **Stonypath farm**.

According to Will Grant, in *The Call of the Pentlands*, the building at **Fairslacks** (NT152545) was so named because the blacksmith at the smiddy (smithy) that once stood here, when asked how things were going, replied, 'Things are fair slack, fair slack', and the smith's nickname became the farm name.

If you have a dog, ensure it is on a lead, as this is a working farm with sheep and cattle. Also be prepared for mud, particularly after wet weather.

7 At Stonypath turn right, signposted to Little Vantage (via Baddinsgill and the Cauldstane Slap) 7½ miles. Walk up the track through the farmyard and take the gate to the right. ◄

At a bend in the track at NT137538, carry straight on along the track and contour round the west side of **Faw Mount**, as it overlooks **Lyne Water**. Keep on the track, which is well used by horses and boggy in places, until you reach a prominent drystane dyke. At this point follow the sign saying 'walkers' and cut down a narrow path to the left.

The path drops down into the cleuch, crossing a couple of wooden boardwalks before picking up the bank of the infant Lyne Water. Cross a rather rickety footbridge before scrambling up to the road .

8 Head north (right) along the road towards **Baddingsgill Farm** and then up the Old Drove Road, signposted Harperrig via the Cauldstane Slap, reaching the col at Cauldstane Slap after about 3km.

9 If you have any energy left at the col, an excursion to the left up **West Cairn Hill** would complete the day, and add 2km and 119m of ascent to your journey. Otherwise, retrace your outward journey down the path to Little Vantage.

WALK 12
West Linton and Siller Holes

Distance	10km
Ascent	80m
Time	2 hours 40 minutes
Maps	Ordnance Survey Landranger 72
	Ordnance Survey Explorer 344
Start/Finish	West Linton, park in the village.

1 If you arrive by car at **West Linton**, park in the village (the roads are narrow, so please park sensibly), or you can travel here by bus (check with Traveline 0870 608 2608 or MacEwans Coach Services).

There is an information board on the green near St Andrew's Church that gives an insight into local history and provides a map.

The village of West Linton is worth exploring – it has a wealth of history as well as places to eat and drink. The option (at number 4) of linking with Walk 11 to carry on to the Cauldstane Slap and rejoin Walk 12 at Stonypath (number 7) is available, and cuts out the long walk up from the north side of the Cauldstane Slap, or you can continue to Baddinsgill and pick up Walk 15.

The village of **West Linton** is worth exploring in some detail, starting at St Andrew's Church. There has been a church at West Linton from the 12th century, although the present building dates from 1781. The interior of the church and the churchyard are full of interesting stonework. The gravestones, many dating from the 17th century, have skulls and crossbones, hour glasses, and other reminders of mortality. From the church walk back up Main Street to the A702, passing the Clock Tower, built over the old village well. The woman whose unflattering stone effigy is carved on the tower is Lady Gifford – the sculptor was her husband, James Gifford. Another example of his work is a panel on the house opposite the Raemartin Hotel.

St Andrew's Church, West Linton

Reach the A702 by walking from the village green up Main Street. At Manor Garage cross the road and walk up a stony road called The Loan – there is a Tweed Trails sign indicating Carlops via The Loan and The Roman Road.

Mendick Hill from the siller holes

Continue up here for about 1km, passing houses with many architectural styles – including an Art Deco house dating from 1935 – until you join another track that was the old Roman road. There is another signpost here, pointing to Carlops, Baddinsgill via Stonypath.

2 Turn right here, and after about 300m look for the **siller holes**.

> The **siller holes** appear as lumps and bumps on the ground in a grassy field to your right, with a flooded pond just below the area. Siller holes were silver holes or mines. Evidence suggests that lead was mined or smelted here (Lead Law NT145530), but silver was also extracted. Fragments of medieval pottery, leather and textiles have been found, as well as balls of cloth, connected by chains and used as pistons in simple water pumps. Mining may have been undertaken for Melrose Abbey, or the other Borders abbeys, for roofing, windows and water pipes. (Artefacts from this location are on display at the National Museum of Scotland, Chambers Street, Edinburgh.)

3 Just beyond the siller holes there is a track leading to **Stonypath Farm**, again clearly signposted 'Little Vantage (via Baddinsgill and the Cauldstane Slap) 7½ miles'. Walk up the track through the farmyard and take the gate to the right. ▶

Ensure you keep your dog on a lead, as this is a working farm with sheep and cattle. Also be prepared for mud, particularly after wet weather.

81

Once through the gate continue along the track, enjoying pleasant views south over **Lyne Water**. At a bend in the track at NT137538 carry straight on along the track and contour round the west side of **Faw Mount** as it overlooks Lyne Water. Keep on the track until you reach a prominent drystane dyke.

At this point follow the sign saying 'walkers' and cut down a narrow path to the left. The path drops down into the cleuch, crossing a couple of wooden boardwalks before picking up the bank of the infant Lyne Water. Cross a rather rickety footbridge before scrambling up to the road.

4 Here a SRWS signpost indicates West Linton, although you have the option of heading up to the Cauldstane Slap to ascend East Cairn Hill and visit the Bore Stane, North Esk Reservoir and Carlops before rejoining the route at Stonypath (see Walk 11) or an ascent of West Cairn Hill, Craigengar and Byrehope Mount (see Walk 15).

5 To stay with Walk 12, go down the metalled road towards West Linton. Pass a house called **Wakefield** on your left. After 2km you will see **West Linton Golf Course** to the right through some trees.

At a junction where a road goes off to the left, there is a signpost indicating West Linton ½ mile or Carlops 2½ miles. The more pleasant option is to take the narrow lane (signposted Carlops 2½ miles), which crosses a fine stone bridge over Lyne Water, passing lovely **Lynedale House** to the right.

Go over the stone bridge and walk up the lane, and at the brow of the rise, amongst some rhododendron bushes, there is a kissing gate, well concealed. Go through the kissing gate and a tight path meanders through mixed woodland, with some fine beech trees hugging the upper side of the glen. ◄

The path eventually emerges, after the descent of a flight of steps, just adjacent to the Manor Garage, opposite the Gordon Arms in West Linton.

The lower part of the woodland is in the care of the Woodland Trust and is aptly named the Catwalk.

WALK 13
Roman Road

Distance	14km
Ascent	110m
Time	3 hours 40 minutes
Maps	Ordnance Survey Landranger 72
	Ordnance Survey Explorer 344
Start/Finish	West Linton Golf Club NT142523

1 Begin the walk at a small lay-by near the entrance to **West Linton Golf Club** (NT142523). Walk left (west) along the road towards **North Slipperfield Farm**.

This is a great walk through a variety of landscapes with historical interest and wildlife to spice it up. It shows another facet of the character of the Pentlands.

Just off to the right, about 250m from the lay-by, there is a small grassy knoll. Laid out on the mound are **early Bronze Age burial chambers** (cists), brought from West Water Reservoir after an excavation in 1992. These cists contained the remains of early farming people, some cremated, others buried, sometimes with objects such as pottery, stone tools or a bead necklace.

There is an interpretation panel here about the Roman road, burial cists and the cairns.

Rejoin the road, and after about 100m fork left at a corner where there is a signpost to Dolphinton 4 miles Mendick Hill 2 miles. ◄ Follow the grassy path ahead, which can be muddy in places, and is the route of a Roman road.

Both DG Moir and Will Grant (1927) (see bibliography) write at length about the **Roman road** and its origins. The highlights are the fact that the road was probably constructed around 80AD by the legions under the command of Agricola. The old Biggar road, which was the main highway until the present road was built in 1833, has many historical connections too. The road would have been busy with pilgrims travelling from

Roman road

South of Mendick Hill on the Roman road

Edinburgh to the shrine of St Ninian at Whithorn in Dumfriesshire. James IV was a frequent traveller and royal accounts record many payments to various alehouses along the route.

Going along the grassy path, pass through the first of a series of gates and cross the stone bridge over **West Water**, which has the distinction of being erected in 1620 and restored in 1899. This was part of an old turnpike road.

2 South Slipperfield Cottages are on your left; continue past these and on to **Hardgatehead** (a ruined cottage), with **Mendick Hill** to the north.

It is perhaps difficult to believe that capercaillie once frequented the **Hardgatehead** area. In *The Breezy Pentlands*, GM Reith records seeing 'a hen-capercailzie' while walking here, and this is corroborated by I Munro, who in *The Birds of the Pentland Hills* mentions capercaillie at Dolphinton and the Peeblesshire border.

3 At the end of Hardgatehead plantation go through a gate, and at NT126500 you can divert to make a short but steep ascent of Mendick Hill. The faint path up Mendick Hill is signposted to your right. It is 181m of ascent from the track to the summit triangulation pillar at 451m, but well worth the effort on a clear day. Return to the track and stay on it – being a former Roman road, it's quite straight! The OS map indicates the course of the Roman road, but our route keeps to the track.

4 Go through some more gates and past **Ingraston** farm, and after about 500m, a quarry at **Sandy Hill**. Follow the Tweed Trails marker post and keep on the track, passing a whitewashed cottage on the left. Go straight ahead, keeping to the edge of a field on the track, and through a gate onto a narrow lane. Go straight along the lane to a minor road, where you go right.

Upper Cairn

5 When you reach the road leading to **Garvald** (opposite Garvald Quarry), turn right and continue on this until you reach **Garvald Home Farm** steading, where there is a signpost indicating West Linton 4 miles. ▸

Take the track off to your right (signposted West Linton 4 miles), going up towards the house at **Medwynbank** through a pair of stone pillars. When the track divides, go right along a track between two more pillars with the name **Ferniehaugh**.

Walk up the track to a small lake and keep heading uphill to the north of a conifer plantation. Keep on the grassy track as it climbs gradually to more open ground, with the glen of **Garvald Burn** to your right. From the track there are good views across to **The Bell** and Mendick Hill.

To the north of the track is **Nether Cairn**, the first of two large cairns of unknown origin. JR Baldwin (see bibliography) remarks that it is one of a series of nine round burial cairns clustered around the 280m contour. Nether Cairn is approximately 15m in diameter and 3.7m high. These cairns may form a chain linking an important prehistoric route from the upper Clyde valley to the Forth estuary. 'It would have left the Clyde at its junction with the Medwin Water, skirted the southwest of the Pentlands and then followed their southwest flanks before cutting across to the River North Esk – where similar cairns existed near Roslin and Rosewell.'

Continue on the track past **Upper Cairn** and **Rumbling Well**, the source of Garvald Burn. Keep on the path, passing a fishing lake on your right and a rough track leading to West Water Reservoir on the left.

6 The path goes past **North Slipperfield Farm**, and at a gate enters West Linton Golf Course. This makes for a very pleasant end to the walk as you rejoin the road back to the start at the golf club.

There is the option here to divert to the Covenanter's Grave and return via Slipperfield Mount and North Slipperfield (see Walk 14).

WALK 14
Covenanters and Cairns

Distance	18km
Ascent	180m
Time	4 hours 50 minutes
Maps	Ordnance Survey Landranger 72
	Ordnance Survey Explorer 344 Pentland Hills
Start/Finish	West Linton Golf Club NT142523

A walk that incorporates two sites of historical interest: Blackhill and the Covenanter's Grave, with the option to visit Roger's Kirk, as well as the prehistoric cairns to the south of North Muir Hill.

1 From a small lay-by next to the entrance to **West Linton Golf Club** (NT142523) walk left (west) along the road in the direction of **North Slipperfield Farm**. The Bronze Age burial cists on a small grassy mound are worthy of a short diversion to your right.

Continue on the road that goes through the golf course and towards **North Slipperfield Farm**. Most of the route goes over land that is used for sheep grazing or grouse moorland, so please exercise responsible access in this area.

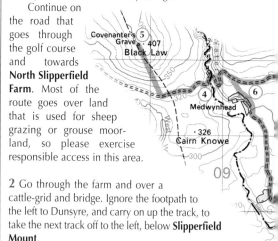

2 Go through the farm and over a cattle-grid and bridge. Ignore the footpath to the left to Dunsyre, and carry on up the track, to take the next track off to the left, below **Slipperfield Mount**.

3 This is a good track marked by a series of metal and wooden posts.

The grassy dam face of **West Water Reservoir** is dominant on your right. West Water was completed in 1967 as a drinking-water supply – it can provide 3.4 million gallons per day. Besides this, it is an internationally important winter roost for pink-footed geese, a regionally important site for common gulls and a site for breeding waders such as dunlin and ringed plover.

Keep left as the track divides (the right fork goes to West Water Reservoir) and continue walking along this track, still marked by large posts. ▶ After about 2km cross a cattle-grid and ford a burn, close together. To the left is a small conifer plantation enclosing the house at **Medwynhead**, and the track folds around on itself and crosses a bridge over **Medwin Water**.

Just after crossing Medwin Water there is the option to divert north and follow another track along the west side of the river to reach the rocky cleuch at **Roger's Kirk** (marked on OS 344 at NT087528). This remote spot was said to be a place where conventicles (illegal gatherings of Covenanters, see Walk 11) were held. Given

The area is open and exposed, and you may hear and see curlews, skylarks and buzzards, each with its evocative call or song adding to the atmosphere of this walk.

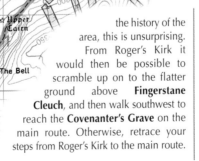

the history of the area, this is unsurprising. From Roger's Kirk it would then be possible to scramble up on to the flatter ground above **Fingerstane Cleuch**, and then walk southwest to reach the **Covenanter's Grave** on the main route. Otherwise, retrace your steps from Roger's Kirk to the main route.

4 Continuing on the main route, you come to the site of a former cottage at **Blackhill** (NT088516).

In 1666 the cottage at Blackhill was the home of a shepherd, **Adam Sanderson**. These were times of insurgents and rebels, the Covenanters, fleeing from the aftermath of the uprising at Rullion Green. One such man was John Carphin, from Ayrshire, wounded in the battle. Carphin was fearful of reprisals to those who harboured fugitives, and also of dying away from the sight of the Ayrshire hills. He refused help and struggled on until he died, at a place Sanderson called Oaken Bush. The shepherd carried him to a spot on Black Hill, where there is a gap to the Ayrshire hills in the southwest, and laid him to rest. This is the place called the Covenanter's Grave.

5 The Covenanter's Grave can be tricky to locate. From the main track another stony track has been constructed on the west side of West Water Burn. Where these meet at NT078516, ascend up through the heather and grass towards a wooden post with a white-painted top. This marks a grouse butt built into the hillside. From the butt continue on up the hill towards a line of tall wooden sight posts on the brow of the hill. The Covenanter's Grave is located at NT077523, in the heather within sight of the Ayrshire Hills, which can be seen through a gap between **Bleak Law** and **Mid Hill**.

The stone at the **Covenanter's Grave** was erected in 1841 at the instigation of Dr Manuel, minister of Dunsyre. The inscription reads, 'Sacred to the memory of a Covenanter who fought and was wounded at Rullion Green Nov 28th 1666 and who died at Oaken Bush the day after the Battle and was buried here by Adam Sanderson of Blackhill.'

Descend by the same route and rejoin the track from Medwin Water.

6 Head back along the track, crossing Medwin Water and with the trees surrounding Medwynhead on your right. Go past the end of a plantation and leave the track just beyond a gate. Pick up a faint ATV track and cross boggy ground around the periphery of the fence until you reach a track going due south to the trees at **Locket Gate Wood** (see OS 344).

Keep on this track as it goes left past another small wood. At the buildings at **Medwynbank** keep left through the farm steading and come out opposite a lake. From the lake take the track that goes to the left, uphill alongside yet another conifer plantation.

7 Stay on this track, passing **Nether Cairn** and **Upper Cairn** (see Walk 13 for details of the cairns), and rejoining the track through **North Slipperfield Farm** and West Linton golf course to return to the start point.

The Covenanter's Grave

WALK 15
Walking with Wolves

Distance	15km
Ascent	465m
Time	4 hours 35 minutes
Maps	Ordnance Survey Landranger 72
	Ordnance Survey Explorer 344
Start/Finish	Baddinsgill NT125549

A walk with a good variety of scenery, from a wooded valley to some open moorland over the Thieves' Road. In 1889 WA Smith, in *The Pentland Hills: Their Paths and Passes*, said, 'It is a delightful contrast to the wild moorland above, and the eye and mind are peculiarly gratified by the peaceful change of scene.'

1 Start this walk at **Baddinsgill** (NT125549). The start point is reached from **West Linton**, north along Medwin Road, an unclassified road from the A702. Parking is limited, so be considerate and do not block gates or impede farm or residents' access.

At Baddinsgill take the Old Drove Road that heads north towards **Baddinsgill Reservoir**. When you cross a small burn, note the fine specimens of beech, larch and Scots pine here. The reservoir appears on your right as the landscape starts to open out.

Go through a metal gate next to a wooden sign indicating Little Vantage via the Cauldstane Slap 5M. Continue uphill on the track and go through another metal gate, leaving the plantations behind and taking to the open ground. After 100m there is a fork to the left towards the south of Muckle Knock. Ignore this and carry on following a Tweed Trails wooden post.

After another 700m the track divides again and there is a Tweed Trails post to direct you to the uphill path. (The right fork leads to Little Hill, do not follow this.) Keep on the track as it crosses **Ravendean Burn** by a small wooden footbridge, heading for the **Cauldstane Slap**.

There are numerous **rocky outcrops** on the 2km between the Ravendean Burn crossing and the

Cauldstane Slap, and it is not difficult to imagine their use as pulpits for conventicles held secretly in the 17th century. In *The Breezy Pentlands* (see bibliography) GM Reith describes the pass as follows, 'Very wild and sombre is the Slap, and if the day be grey, as it is so often in our brumous isle, and if the clouds are flying low, scraping the sides of the hills, it looks desolate in the extreme. We are miles away from the nearest human habitation. Looking northward from the ridge, we have a view whose soft beauties are in strong contrast to the bleak ruggedness of our immediate surroundings.'

2 At the Cauldstane Slap there is a metal gate and a large wooden stile to cross the fence, but we stay on the south side. (There is also a signpost pointing north to Little Vantage 2½M and back south to West Linton 5M – ignore both these signs.)

3 Following the fence, head off left on a rough path up the boggy slopes of **West Cairn Hill**. The fence is eventually replaced by a fine example of the art of the drystane dyker. Keep on the path alongside this dyke as it turns at right angles to the summit at 562m, marked by an Ordnance Survey triangulation pillar and a small cairn.

Cloudberry grows in abundance on the way up to West Cairn Hill. It is a plant that along with blaeberry, heather and cross-leaved heath is characteristic of **boggy and peaty uplands**. W Anderson (see bibliography) found cloudberry commonly at the Cheviot,

Cloudberry

Wolf Craigs

where it was called 'noops' and made into a delicious jelly. He also records that the plant is found in Norway, where it is known as ground mulberry and eaten both raw and preserved. Various vivid green and red sphagnum mosses, shrubby lichens and sedges also grow here, making it a colourful place.

4 Leave the summit of West Cairn Hill on a path and head left (southwest) along the flattish ridge of **Cloven Craig**, keeping alongside a dyke and fence for about 300m until they turn away northwest. Continue on the path along to **Colzium Hill**.

5 At Colzium Hill an ATV track is useful as you continue along the broad ridge, boggy in places, but making for easy walking on the soft heathery ground. Continue

95

along the track until you reach a stock fence. Follow this fence line, heading downhill (southeast).

The stone gargoyles and weird shapes of Wolf Craigs give an eerie atmosphere, and the rock formations are reminiscent of Dartmoor's granite tors.

6 At the bottom of a boggy area go left, where you will see the rocky cleft called **Wolf Craigs**. ◄ At Wolf Craigs cross the fence and climb south, with the fence on your left, over heathery and fairly boggy ground, to reach a post with a bright-orange marker and the number 395 on the top.

Just beyond the post is a narrow wooden footbridge over **West Water Burn**. Go over the bridge and over the metal gate at NT097555. From here walk southwest to a prominent cairn.

7 Walk to a second cairn, about 50m away, and then west for 400m to the summit cairn at **Craigengar**, at 519m. From the summit of Craigengar walk back down the slope, keeping the fence that you came through at the metal gate to your left, to cross West Water burn again.

Part of **Craigengar** has been designated a site of special scientific interest (SSSI) for its upland plants, and part of the area is also designated a special area of conservation (SAC) for its large population of marsh saxifrage. This is an uncommon plant that is becoming increasingly scarce due to overgrazing and drainage. Adjacent to the summit of Craigengar are several rocks with various names and dates etched onto them. The dates range from April 1888 to 1933 and feature the name Dunlop.

8 After crossing West Water Burn, climb up alongside another fence. Climb over a wooden gate to the other side of the fence, keeping to the left side of this fence. Follow the fence east then at right angles southeast, on faint path towards the ridge of **Byrehope Mount**. Keep alongside the left of this fence until you reach the rounded top of Byrehope Mount (536m). From Byrehope Mount keep to the left side of the fence as it follows a path downhill.

Pass a fence and gate to your right and note **Baddinsgill Reservoir** ahead and **West Water Reservoir** to the right. The fence is soon replaced by a dyke as you continue downhill on the path over easy ground. Near the bottom of the hill, at NT123546, there are some ruined dykes overgrown with vegetation – step over these and use a stile to cross a fence into **Dipper Wood**.

Walk left alongside a dyke (with large gaps in it) in the woodland. At the bottom of this slope there's a path that goes round the wood. Go through a gate and turn left here to walk along a path with a field to the left and wooded **Glen Ely** to the right.

At the end of this path there is another wooden gate leading out onto a road. Turn left here and return to the start of the walk.

Carvings on rocks at Craigengar

WALK 16
Poets and Witches

Distance	8km
Ascent	185m
Time	2 hours 20 minutes
Maps	Ordnance Survey Landranger 72
	Ordnance Survey Explorer 344
Start/Finish	Carlops NT161558

This walk offers much of geomorphological, natural and historical interest, as well as good views in clear weather. This walk can be linked with Walk 11 to make a longer route.

1 The walk begins at **Carlops**. There is a small car park opposite the newly built village hall, or you can reach Carlops by public transport (MacEwen's Coach Services, number 100, tel Traveline on 0870 608 2608).

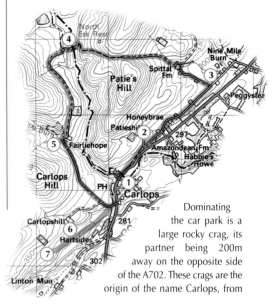

Dominating the car park is a large rocky crag, its partner being 200m away on the opposite side of the A702. These crags are the origin of the name Carlops, from

Carlin's Leap, the story being that a carline, or witch, lived nearby and was often seen leaping between the crags on her broomstick. The witches in question were Jenny Barry, who inhabited the cave you will visit later (number 7), and another woman called Mause who lived at Kittley Brig.

The hamlet of Carlops is described in depth by GM Reith and DG Moir (see bibliography). Much of its historical significance springs from a romantic pastoral comedy called *The Gentle Shepherd*, written by **Allan Ramsay** and published in 1725, and set in and around Carlops. Reith notes, 'The scenery of this mystic drama is Habbie's Howe and the neighbourhood of Carlops generally. Through his *Gentle Shepherd* Ramsay has become a kind of godfather to the farms and landmarks of the whole district, for there are to be seen here and there over the countryside places bearing names such as these – Patie's Hill and Patie's Mill, Roger's Rig, Jenny's Brae, Peggy's Lea, The Lonely Bield, etc.'

Starting from the **Allan Ramsay Hotel**, walk through the village alongside the busy A702 in the direction of Edinburgh, i.e. northeast. Pass a bus stop, a spring and water trough, and a SWRS sign indicating Buteland by the Bore Stane 5½M, pointing up a narrow lane on your left. Continue past the lane and along the road for about

Allan Ramsay Hotel, Carlops

another 100m, and just after crossing into Midlothian there is a sign indicating Nine Mile Burn, up a flight of steps to the left.

2 Go up the steps and onto a narrow path that climbs up above the road on the south side of **Patie's Hill**, and past a bench giving a good view over to **Habbie's Howe**, a wooded valley mentioned by Ramsay. After about 300m the path joins an unclassified road. Continue along the road for another 300m to **Wanton Wa's** cottage. At the cottage keep left and walk along this road for a further kilometre. The views of the hills here are superb.

3 Turn left at a SWRS sign indicating Buteland by N Esk Reservoir and walk up the track towards **Spittal Farm**. Keep on the track as it bends right and passes some farm buildings. Before the track bends to the left, go right through a gate with a waymarking arrow on it (the ground here may be quite muddy).

From the gate keep on the track and follow way-marking arrows left over a stile and through another gate. Go left on a track that crosses a small burn and heads uphill steeply. There are two further gates and a stile to negotiate, but the views are worth the effort. Continue on the track alongside a line of fenceposts marked with arrows to the top of the hill.

4 Follow the path down to the left and on to **North Esk Reservoir** (for information about the reservoir, see Walk 11). (At North Esk Reservoir there is the option to follow part of Walk 11 anti-clockwise, via the Bore Stane, East Cairn Hill, the Cauldstane Slap, Baddingsgill, Stonypath and Carlops. This would add 14km, 240m of ascent and 4 hours to your walk, making for a full day.) Cross a stile at the bottom of the hill by the reservoir and then walk along the top of the dam to the former water-keeper's cottage. From the cottage take a rough track that goes straight ahead then bends left in a southerly direction back towards Carlops via **Fairliehope**. A signpost next to the cottage indicates Carlops.

North Esk Reservoir was designed by the civil engineers Fox Adamson, for whom Robert Louis Stevenson's father worked, and Stevenson's name often appeared in the register of visitors kept at the water-keeper's cottage. John Tod, 'the Roarin' Shepherd' of Stevenson's acquaintance, had a son, Willie, who also became a shepherd. However, he was later employed as the water-keeper and discovered the burial cists that were revealed when the water level in the reservoir fell in 1905 (see Walk 11). This is an area frequented by brown hares, and you also have a good chance of seeing buzzards and kestrels too.

5 Continue on down the track past the house and steading at Fairliehope on your left.

The shepherdess **Jenny Armstrong** was born at Fairliehope in 1903. Jenny, her work and the landscapes around here were the subject of paintings and drawings by the distinguished artist Victoria Crowe, who lived nearby at Kitleyknowe. An exhibition of this work was displayed at the Scottish National Portrait Gallery in 2000 and published as a book, *A Shepherd's Life*.

The route keeps going downhill to cross a small bridge over **Fairliehope Burn**, where there is another signpost indicating Carlops car park, before climbing again. Keep on this track for another kilometre, passing another track to the right to Carlophill Farm, and about 300m later you will see a kissing gate to your right, just above the cottages in Carlops.

Go through this gate and across the field, then over a small bridge crossing a burn below the farm, towards another kissing gate just after the burn. From this kissing gate head left, over to four wooden posts and electric fencing just by **Dun Kaim**, part of the ridge formed by glacial deposits. Either climb on a path to the top of the ridge and walk southwest to its end, or walk around its perimeter, keeping to the drier south side. (Dun Kaim is marked on OS 344.)

Dun Kaim, near Carlops

6 At the end of the ridge follow a path across to another ridge, called **Peaked Craig**.

7 **Jenny Barry's Cove**, or Hell's Hole, is located in the hillside by a spring, about 50m from the end of Peaked Craig to the right.

The area between Carlophill and Hartside is known as **Carlops Dean** at the eastern end and **Windy Gowl** at the western end, and the unusual landforms were first written about by Milne Home in 1840. These features were formed when melting ice from the Southern Uplands cut channels into the bedrock in a braided pattern, joining and rejoining, with a number of rock 'islands' in the larger channels. There is also a long, sinuous, broken ridge of sands and gravels, called an 'esker', running down the centre. The names here are marvellous – Seven Cauldrons, Hell's Hole and Hollow Haugh. Because of its wealth of geomorphological features, the area was designated a site of special scientific interest (SSSI) in 1975. (For more information refer to Quaternary of Scotland (1993) edited by Gordon and Sutherland.)

After visiting the cove, return to the track by the same route, turn right at the kissing gate and descend a few metres back to your starting point in **Carlops**.

WALK 17
North Esk Valley

Distance	7km
Ascent	210m
Time	2 hours 10 minutes
Maps	Ordnance Survey Landranger 65
	Ordnance Survey Explorer 344
Start/Finish	Carlops NT161558

1 Begin the walk in **Carlops**, either at the small car park opposite the village hall or from the bus stop in the centre of the village. Walk in a northerly direction through the village, along its main street, the A702, heading towards Edinburgh. Just beyond a bus stop and a water trough, cross the road and head along a narrow lane, signposted Buteland by the Bore Stane 5½M.

This is a lovely walk, full of variety and contrast. It begins in a beautiful secluded glen, and then opens out to cross a grassy hillside with magnificent views along the Pentland ridge.

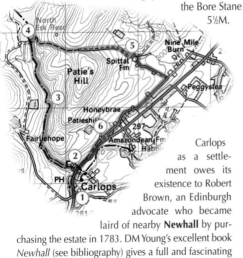

Carlops as a settlement owes its existence to Robert Brown, an Edinburgh advocate who became laird of nearby **Newhall** by purchasing the estate in 1783. DM Young's excellent book *Newhall* (see bibliography) gives a full and fascinating history of this country estate. Carlops was transformed into a community of cotton weavers, and the original whitewashed cottages are still the main fabric of the village, although the looms ceased to function in 1894.

2 The lane goes down to Patie's Mill and **Carlops Bridge**, a lovely secluded spot, and instantly away from the busy traffic. Go through a wooden kissing gate by a beech hedge to the right of Patie's Mill house, and take the path that runs alongside the beech hedge to another gate.

At **Carlops Bridge** look out for dippers or grey wagtails by the water's edge. The grey wagtail is strongly associated with fast-flowing burns. The male in spring colours is a bright palette of yellow breast, black bib and slate-grey back. The grey wagtail has the longest tail of the three British species, which it bobs up and down constantly.

Carlops Bridge

3 Go through the gate and the path leads out to a more open grassy area beside the infant **River North Esk**, at the start of the **North Esk Valley**.

This walk is excellent for **wildflowers** in season, and species such as few-flowered spike rush, fragrant orchid, globeflower and mountain everlasting are found here. In 1988 the valley was designated a site of special scientific interest (SSSI) for its rich flora and geological interest.

The route follows a path along the burn and is narrow, steep and slippery in places, and care must be taken here. There are also a number of places where the path forks, but keep heading upstream.

After about 1.5km you come upon a ruin, now just the outlines of the walls of a small building, called **Back Spittal** (NT157574). GM Reith (see bibliography) suggests it may have been constructed by the Cistercian monks of Newhall as a sort of isolation unit for patients in their care, who were lepers or suffering from small pox.

4 Stay on this, the northeast side of the burn, for approximately 500m until you reach the dam at **North Esk Reservoir**. Take some time to enjoy the view over the reservoir, and perhaps read the interpretation boards about the reservoir, provided by the Pentland Hills Regional Park. Return to the stile at the end of the dam and ascend steeply up the hillside on a path in a westerly direction.

5 Continue on the path as it then descends down to **Spittal Farm**. Go round to the left of the farm and take the track that leads down to an unclassified road, where there is a signpost indicating Carlops.

GM Reith (see bibliography) says, 'The name **Spittal** is fairly common in Scotland, and usually marks the site either of a wayside refuge for pilgrims and other travellers, or of a lazar [leper] house, erected and maintained by some monkish fraternity.' The monks may have been the Cistercian brothers of Newhall and they established a hospital in the locality. To the east is a small patch of land called **St Robert's Croft**. St Robert was a Benedictine monk who founded the congregation of Cistercians in 1098.

6 Turn right along the road, passing Beechbank, **Honeybrae** and Wanton Wa's cottage. At Wanton Wa's go straight along the road to a sharp bend. The road continues up to Patieshill, but at the bend you go left to the path that runs above the A702 and eventually joins the main road after about 500m. Walk back into Carlops to your starting point.

View over North Esk Reservoir from the replica shooting butt

WALK 18
The Monks' Road

Distance	6km
Ascent	215m
Time	1hour 50 minutes
Maps	Ordnance Survey Landranger 65
	Ordnance Survey Explorer 344
Start/Finish	Nine Mile Burn NT177577

1 Begin the walk at **Nine Mile Burn**, a hamlet of a few houses at NT177577. Nine Mile Burn is so named because it is 9 Scots miles (11¾ English miles) from Edinburgh. There are a few parking spaces available here.

From the signpost at the car park declaring 'Balerno by Monks Rig and Braid Law 6M', go through a wooden kissing gate adjacent to a field gate next to the car park. The ground is sometimes very muddy and poached up by cattle, so if necessary pick your way across, or follow the path by the dyke around the field edge, straight ahead, to another signpost for Monks Rig and Braid Law.

A short but very sweet walk, it has a lovely wild feeling and the added mystery of the Font Stane, as well as some wind-sculpted trees and good vistas over the ridge.

107

At this signpost go uphill on the path alongside the dyke for about 300m until you reach a stile and a signpost indicating Nine Mile Burn. After crossing the stile go immediately right by the drystane dyke to yet another signpost, about 500m away, to **Monks Rig**.

2 The path follows the fence and passes a gate in a slight hollow before gradually going uphill. Monks Burn flows through the lovely sheltered cleuch to the left. Still on the path, cross the fence at the stile (about 200m from the hollow) and cut across diagonally to another stile, where patches of soft rush (*Juncus effusus*) grow. ◄

Go over this stile too and cross a tumbled-down dyke next to it. There is a clear and obvious grassy track leading uphill from here. The path follows the route of the **Monk's Road**, probably part of a well-worn track between the monastery at Newhall and the abbey at Dunfermline, across the Firth of Forth, by way of Queensferry.

3 The ground rises gradually on the good path, and after about 500m you will see a shallow stone trough – the **Font Stane** – next to the path, probably containing a few coins.

GM Reith, W Grant (see bibliography) and others speculate on the origins of the **Font Stane**. 'Whether it was a Font Stone, a wayside shrine, or a landmark commanding all the country to the south for the pious friar as he journeyed over the hills to Convent or Spital, who can tell? but there it remains to-day, and as we stand and meditate upon it we link ourselves with a visible symbol of the time when the white-robed monk was a familiar figure on the Pentland Hills.' W Grant, *The Call of the Pentlands*.

4 Pass the Font Stane and continue on the good path along the grassy ridge over **Cap Law**, to join another path near the foot of **West Kip**. There is a signpost here for Nine Mile Burn by Monk's Rig.

Rushes of course are indicators of boggy ground, and are good cover for birds such as meadow pipits, skylarks and jack snipe.

The Ranger Service was contacted by the Ordnance Survey when they were in the process of revising their Explorer map for the Pentland Hills. It was pointed out that the hill has been mistakenly named **Cap Law** for many years, probably due to a typographical error in a Bartholomew's map, and that the original name is Gap Law. However, the Ordnance Survey has decided to use the name in most common usage today, i.e. Cap Law.

Turn right along the path, and after a few metres take another path that goes off to the right again, beside a wire fence. The path skirts below a scrubby plantation and enjoys a good view down the valley of the **Eastside Burn**, with the Kips as a backdrop.

5 Stay on the path as it goes south, and take the right fork where the path forks to go to the west side of **Braid Law**. Descend here quite steeply and ford a small burn before rising again across grassy ground. Cross a drystane dyke and walk steadily downhill for about 600m to reach another stile.

Cross the stile and follow the field edge downhill to your left, turning the corner at right angles at the bottom of the field to reach a gate and a stile. Climb the stile and go straight ahead until you reach another stile and a signpost pointing to Nine Mile Burn. Cross this stile and walk downhill, turning right at the bottom of the field to go through the kissing gate at **Nine Mile Burn** car park.

The Font Stane

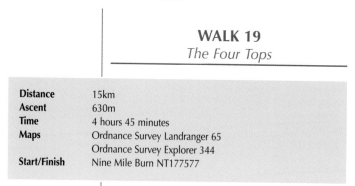

WALK 19
The Four Tops

Distance	15km
Ascent	630m
Time	4 hours 45 minutes
Maps	Ordnance Survey Landranger 65
	Ordnance Survey Explorer 344
Start/Finish	Nine Mile Burn NT177577

This is an extension of Walk 18 and includes the four tops of East and West Kip, Scald Law and South Black Hill. (It also offers an alternative starting point to Walk 9, as the Nine Mile Burn approach to the four tops is more convenient if coming from the east of Edinburgh.)

This walk has a fairly gentle start, then a short sharp pull up West Kip, followed by the excellent roller coaster over the tops and down to Green Cleuch. The route finishes with another short ascent to skirt the south side of Hare Hill, before recrossing Logan Burn and returning to Nine Mile Burn.

1 Begin the walk at the hamlet of **Nine Mile Burn** (NT177577 – as for Walk 18) and go through a kissing gate next to a field gate, signposted Balerno by Monks Rig and Braid Law 6M. Go uphill on the path alongside the dyke for about 300m until you reach a stile and a signpost indicating Nine Mile Burn. After crossing the stile go immediately right by the drystane dyke to yet another signpost about 50m away.

2 Take the path uphill signed to **Monks Rig**. Follow the fence, passing a gate in a slight hollow and then going gradually uphill. Still on the path, cross the fence at a stile about 200m from the hollow, then cut across diagonally to another stile and a fallen-down drystane dyke. Go over these too and follow an obvious grassy track leading uphill. Walk along this track for about 500m until you pass the **Font Stane** on your right.

3 Continue on the path over the ridge of **Cap Law** for another kilometre before reaching the foot of West Kip.

There is a signpost here indicating Nine Mile Burn by Monk's rig. (We also join Walk 10 here.)

4 Ascend **West Kip** – it is a short but steep pull, with many grassy steps in the hillside formed by the footsteps of walkers. Enjoy the undulating ridge walk.

5 Continue straight ahead on the path along the ridge in the direction of **East Kip** (there is a small dip between West Kip and East Kip). Descend East Kip on the path and at **Cross Sward** (NT187608 – the lower ground between East Kip, Scald Law and South Black Hill) you have the option of swinging away right (south-west) on a path for the 600m to the summit of **South Black Hill**.

6 There is a small stone cairn on the summit of South Black Hill (NT191605).

7 Return to the path, and when it divides follow the right fork for 750m to the highest point in the Pentlands, **Scald Law**, 579m, marked by a trig pillar.

The origin of the name **Scald Law** is the subject of some debate. W Anderson (see bibliography) favoured 'poet's hill', from the Scandinavian for 'a reciter', and this is corroborated by Will Grant in *The Call of the Pentlands*. However, JR Baldwin (see bibliography) suggests it is

*View from Scald Law
trig point*

from the local word for 'bramble', although none are to be found growing here.

After enjoying the view from Scald Law, descend on the stony path straight ahead (northeast) and down to the bealach between Scald Law and **Carnethy**. The path zigzags downhill, with a series of water bars and cross drains bisecting it to direct water from its surface and prevent further erosion. The Ranger Service has spent time and money tackling the erosion caused by so many boots on the relatively fragile and thin soils on this and other hills.

At the bealach turn left (north) on a stony path, at first by a dyke and fence. After about 200m cross the fence by a ladder stile and walk down the path on to more open grassy areas (with **Loganlea Reservoir** to the right), looking ahead to Black Hill and left down to **Green Cleuch**. ◀

The former shepherd's house standing to your right, at the head of Loganlea Reservoir, is the Howe.

The **rocks** in this area are the oldest in the Pentlands, dating from the Silurian period, 435 million years ago. The rock beds are nearly vertical and are bands of sandstone and mudstone. They were folded and moulded probably during the Caledonian orogeny (a period of violent movements of the Earth's crust).

8 From the open grassy area turn left and walk along a grassy path into Green Cleuch, the deep cleft between Black Hill and Hare Hill.

The fenced area to your left below the crags on the south side of the cleuch is a SSSI known for its rare plants and mosses. The fencing protects the plants from grazing sheep. Within the fenced area is Logan Burn waterfall, spectacular after heavy rain.

9 Stay on the path and keep to the left until after 300m you reach a wooden footbridge. Cross the burn by this bridge and remain on the now stony path that hugs the base of Black Hill. Keep on the path until after about 500m you see another stony path winding its way up through the bracken on the left (west) side of Green Cleuch, at NT182621. The path is quite steep at first, and somewhat peaty and boggy in places, but flattens out as it reaches the heathery slopes of **Hare Hill**. ▶

10 Follow this path for about a kilometre as it traverses the side of Hare Hill, then meets up with a broad path that connects Balerno and Nine Mile Burn. At the broad path turn left (south) and make towards the foot of West Kip. The path crosses **Logan Burn** (which forms the waterfall you passed earlier) by a well-built stone bridge.

Ascend gradually to the base of West Kip, and after about 20m take a path that drops down to the right and skirts the plantation on **Cap Law** (ignore the wide track that goes down to Eastside). ▶

11 Follow the path as it contours round Cap Law, passing two conifer plantations on the right, then walk south to head down the west side of **Braid Law**. Cross the infant Quarrel Burn at NT180593 and keep to the path as it skirts the field above Nine Mile Burn. From here rejoin the outward route and follow the signposts back to the start at Nine Mile Burn.

The Hare Hill path is known as the Sweep Road by the Ranger Service, but not so named on any map. It is quite peaty in places and rarely dries out completely, even in good weather.

An alternative is to return along your outward route via Monks Rig, which is signposted at NT174604. The view here is lovely, taking in Eastside and the backdrop of hills.

Green Cleuch from Carnethy

WALK 20
The Carnethy 5

Distance	10km
Ascent	730m
Time	3 hours 30 minutes
Maps	Ordnance Survey Landranger 66
	Ordnance Survey Explorer 344
Start/Finish	Kirk Road end lay-by NT211607

This route follows the course of the Carnethy 5 Hill Race, organised annually by the Carnethy Hill Running Club to commemorate the Battle of Roslin, fought in February 1302 between Sir William Wallace and an English army. The fastest hill runners complete the race in about 45 minutes. (Visit www.carnethy.com for the history of the race, as well as entry details if you are feeling fit).

It is easy to see why this route is so popular with runners as well as walkers – it is very much in the heart of the Pentlands, and particularly good when the heather is in full bloom.

1 Begin at the **Kirk Road** lay-by on the A702, at NT211607, about 1km north of **Silverburn**. Spaces here are limited and the traffic tends to be fast, so care is needed in both pulling into and exiting the lay-by. (If it is full, there is another lay-by further down the A702, on the opposite side of the road.)

From the lay-by go through a wooden kissing gate. There is a signpost here saying Kirk Road, as well as a SRWS green signpost indicating Balerno 6M, and an obvious path leading into the hills. The first part of the route can be very muddy and damp, so pick your way carefully alongside the fence and dyke on your right to avoid wet feet.

The bulk of Carnethy lies in front to the right and Scald Law to the left. The bealach between them is the route of **the old Kirk Road** (see Walk 10), along which parishioners walked from Logan Valley to Penicuik to attend the kirk.

The path leads into the hills in a generally northwesterly direction. After about 700m you reach a kissing gate at a place called Charlie's Loup (the origin of this name is described on the stone plaque next to the gate). Go through the gate, and from here it is a gradual climb along the lovely heathery side of **Carnethy**, which steepens as the narrow path climbs to the bealach.

2 At the bealach, cross a stile to your left and ascend the stony path that zigzags up **Scald Law**. The Ordnance Survey triangulation pillar at the summit of Scald Law is soon reached. It is the highest point in the Pentland Hills range, at 579m.

Charlie's Loup plaque

The Ranger Service has spent a lot of time **repairing and maintaining the path** up Scald Law, and many other paths in the regional park, mainly by channelling water away. This is done with the use of ditches, cross drains, water bars and French drains, all of which require regular clearing of vegetation, stones and silt. Specialist upland path contractors are used to carry out the work, using local stone where possible. Only essential work is done, principally where the path has widened due to heavy use. Upland environments are very sensitive to

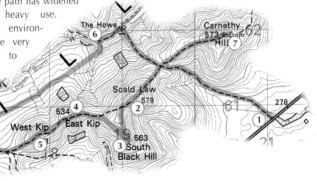

erosion, because of thin soils and harsh weather. Walkers can help to have a minimum impact by keeping to the line of the path, not cutting corners, and kicking out stones where water bars and cross drains have become blocked. Mountain bikers and horse riders can help by choosing routes responsibly – avoid those susceptible to erosion and be especially careful in wet weather.

Walker in Green Cleugh

3 Continue west for 200m on a path along the ridge that goes off the summit of Scald Law. Detour left (southwest) on a peaty path to the cairn on the top of **South Black Hill** before rejoining the path, left, to continue the ridge walk between Scald Law and **East Kip**.

4 Walk on the path over the ridge between East Kip and **West Kip**.

5 Using the grassy steps formed in the hillside by walkers, descend West Kip by its westerly side. At the base of West Kip go right on a grassy track, following the signpost to Balerno. After about 400m go right, parallel to **Logan Burn** (down to your left), over grassy slopes and below the rectangular conifer plantation on the north slopes of East Kip. Keep walking northeast again to below the conifer plantation on Scald Law. There is an ATV track here, at the top of the fencing that keeps sheep out of the SSSI in Green Cleuch (see Walk 19, number 8). ◄

There are great views of Loganlea and Glencorse Reservoirs from here, so take time to enjoy them.

6 Follow the ATV track steeply down towards the sheep fanks (pens) and into **Green Cleuch**. Walk alongside a fence before turning right up a track that is the other part of the Kirk Road, signposted Penicuik and Kirk Road.

7 Ascend to the bealach, this time detouring left on the path up the bulk of **Carnethy Hill** to the cairn at 573m. Return to the bealach and back the way you came, to the start at the lay-by.

WALK 21
Carnethy Canter

Distance	6km
Ascent	294m
Time	2 hours
Maps	Ordnance Survey Landranger 66
	Ordnance Survey Explorer 344
Start/Finish	Kirk Road end lay-by NT211607

1 Begin at the large lay-by at NT211607 on the A702 – see Walk 20. The start of the walk can be very wet and muddy, so pick your way alongside the fence and dyke until the path becomes clearer.

Go through a wooden kissing gate where there is a SRWS signpost indicating Balerno 6M.

This walk can be enjoyed in either direction. The route description is for an anti-clockwise walk, but is probably best walked clockwise if the wind is westerly. The walk is particularly lovely when the heather is in full bloom.

Follow this path until you reach a large wooden post with the word 'footpath', indicating a grassy path north. Walk up this easy path through the bracken towards **Fala Knowe**, keeping right when the path forks. (Fala Knowe is marked on OS 344, but appears as a hillock at NT211616 on OS 66.)

There is another **Fala Knowe** between Castlelaw Hill and Allermuir Hill, at NT226655 (see Route 5). The name derives from the Anglian *fah hlaw*, or Scots *faw law*, meaning 'speckled hill of a cairn like or conical shape'.

Scald Law from the Kirk Road

2 Keep on the grassy path until you reach a dyke, a fence and a stile. Cross the stile and go sharp left to begin a gradual climb through the heather on a rough path that peters out. Keep contouring round the base of Carnethy Hill until you come into the obvious bealach between Carnethy Hill to your left and Turnhouse Hill to your right. You will see a fence and dyke running through the middle of the bealach down to your right. Keep on this left side until you reach the crest of the bealach, with a stile and a gate in the dyke and fence.

3 Go left on the obvious wide, stony path as it pulls south and then west up to the cairns on Carnethy Hill.

It was along this section of path that a walker from Penicuik came upon a decorated **bronze axehead**. After reporting the find to Historic Scotland, the archaeologists were able to say that flat bronze axe-heads of this type were among the items made by the earliest metal workers in Scotland, and that it dated from around 2000BC. As the axehead was richly decorated it was probably ceremonial, rather than a tool for everyday use, and it may have been buried deliberately, perhaps marking a boundary.

Most of the original Bronze Age cairn on Carnethy summit has been destroyed to make a number of small stone shelters.

◄ Continue west on a path from Carnethy summit over ground that is quite peaty in places, but otherwise good going. After about 1km you reach the bealach between Carnethy and **Scald Law**. The heather in this small glen is spectacular when in full bloom.

4 At the bealach turn left and walk downhill on a stony path that sweeps back down through the heather to the kissing gate at Charlie's Loup. Go through the gate and it's only a short, easy 700m to the start point.

WALK 22
History in the Hills

Distance	5km
Ascent	175m
Time	1 hour 30 minutes
Maps	Ordnance Survey Landranger 66
	Ordnance Survey Explorer 344
Start/Finish	Flotterstone car park NT232631

1 The route begins at the car park at **Flotterstone** NT232631, which may be busy at weekends and on holidays. (Parking at Rullion Green is not recommended, as the track to the cottage is narrow and the A702 busy.)

This route takes in the site of the Battle of Rullion Green, fought on 28 November 1666, and also looks at the Martyrs' Monument, some archaeological remains, and the history of a sheep market.

Leave the car park and go west along the private road leading towards **Glencorse Reservoir**. After about 500m take a path off to your left, signposted Scald Law. Go through a wooden gate and along the track for a short distance to a gate and a bridge on the left, again signposted to Scald Law.

2 Go through the gate and over the bridge on a wide path, up onto a bracken-covered rise then over a grassy knoll before beginning the ascent of **Turnhouse Hill**.

121

*Setting off up
Turnhouse Hill*

Cross over a stile and then another, and follow alongside a drystane dyke for a short distance until it turns away left. Leave the path here (NT221630) and follow the dyke as it contours round the slopes of Turnhouse Hill.

3 Still following the dyke, keep on the slope above the trees until the dyke turns sharp left. At this point cross, going through two gates, to reach a hillock about 500m away. The hillock is marked on the map as the location of a prehistoric fort, and some ditches and ramparts are visible on the ground. On 28 November 1666 the main action of the Battle of Rullion Green took place in the hollow between **Lawhead Hill** and this hillock.

The **Battle of Rullion Green** was the culmination of an uprising by Covenanters, a loose grouping of

Presbyterians who refused to accept a kirk ruled by the king and bishops. In appalling weather a band of insurgents marched from Galloway, Ayrshire and Lanark towards Edinburgh. Government troops, under the command of the infamous General Tam Dalziel of the Binns, pursued the rebel force, which numbered about 900 men. The well-trained and -equipped Royalist force, of 3000 cavalry and infantry, caught up with the Covenanters and followed them over the route of Maiden's Cleuch and round to Castlelaw, before clashing on the lower slopes of Turnhouse Hill. It was less of a battle and more of a rout, and the weary, outnumbered and outclassed Covenanters were either killed on the field, taken prisoner, or hunted down as they tried to make their escape through the Pentlands towards Ayrshire and Galloway.

One such fugitive was John Carphin, who although badly wounded, made it as far as Adam Sanderson's cottage at Blackhill, some 20km away. Unfortunately Carphin died of his wounds, and the shepherd buried him within sight of the Ayrshire hills of his home (see Walk 14, Covenanters and Cairns).

There has been some recent debate about the actual site of the battle, based on historical research into the accounts of the skirmish made at the time by soldiers. The maps mark the location approximately 1km *north* of the place now thought to have been the actual battle site.

George Reith's description of the Pentland Rising in *The Breezy Pentlands* is a demonstration of his writing style at its best, and worth reading in full.

Having reflected on the place and its turbulent past, go downhill from the hillock on an ATV track, through a gate, and walk towards the right-hand corner of some trees next to the fence and dyke.

Just before a gate that leads to a narrow corridor where the path goes between a dyke and the plantation (at NT220622), there are some curious depressions in the ground – these are a group of 11 **ring enclosures**. Small deposits of cremated bones were found on pre-pared surfaces within the enclosures, and fragments of charcoal and flint flakes were also found. These were dated to between 600–100BC when excavated in 1983–5. This area is marked on the 1852 Ordnance Survey 6 inch map as a 'Covenanters' Encampment'. Perhaps early historians mistook these earlier remains as evidence of an encampment, given the proximity to the battle site? This 1852 map also places the battle site at an area north of Rullion Green cottage, near to House o' Muir.

Go through the gate and down the narrow corridor between the dyke and the plantation. Descend the path, go through another gate, then turn left and walk along the edge of the trees for about 80m to the Martyrs' Monument, surrounded by blood-red metal railings. A small plaque telling the story of the monument is fixed to the railings.

Walk down across the field towards **Rullion Green cottage**, and go through the gate in front of the cottage before heading along the track leading right to the main road.

4 Turn left down the road (there is a pavement) for about 1km to the group of buildings at **House o' Muir**. There is a gate and a muddy track to the left of the houses, sign-posted 'Glencorse Reservoir' – take this track.

It is difficult to believe that **House o' Muir** was once the site of one of the largest sheep markets in the country. *The New Statistical Account of Scotland for Edinburghshire*, May 1843, records, 'There is an annual market for sheep held at House of Muir on the first and second Mondays of April, to which sheep are sent from various parts of Scotland, and purchasers attend from a great distance.' The 1861 census for House o' Muir returns 24 people, including two ploughmen, a dairy-maid, a shepherd and six sheep drovers. The market also needed an inn to supply the many shepherds and drovers who travelled to the area. The inn, at Marchwell, was run by a Mrs Hunter. The 1852 OS map marks the House of Muir Sheep Market on the field you crossed below the Martyrs' Monument.

Walk down the track, passing through a gate with a fine line of beech trees to your left, and then down a muddy path, to first cross a small burn by a wooden sleeper bridge, then a wooden footbridge over **Glencorse Burn**.

From the footbridge go through the gate and turn right along the path to another gate. Go through the gate, and turn right along the road to return to the car park at the start.

The Martyrs' Monument

WALK 23
Flotterstone and Fala Knowe

Distance	8km (optional ascent of Castlelaw Hill add 1km)
Ascent	230m (optional ascent of Castlelaw Hill add 88m)
Time	2 hours 25 minutes (optional ascent of Castlelaw Hill add 20 minutes)
Maps	Ordnance Survey Landranger 66
	Ordnance Survey Explorer 344
Start/Finish	Flotterstone car park NT232631

Although this walk begins at Flotterstone, it is easy to escape the crowds on the glen road and enjoy great views over the ridge and Midlothian, as well as taking in some history.

CTR Wilson plaque

1 From **Flotterstone** car park, at NT232631, walk past the Flotterstone visitor centre (open daily 9.30am to 4.00pm, displays, leaflets, toilets and disabled access) and along a good path through woodland.

About 200m along the woodland path there is a blue plaque mounted in a stone cairn. The plaque commemorates **CTR Wilson**, who was born at Crosshouse Farm on 14 February 1869, the youngest of eight children of a sheep farmer. Charles Wilson went to Cambridge University and graduated in natural science in 1892. He was a keen hill walker, and on a visit to the observatory on the summit of Ben Nevis, was intrigued by the cloud formations he saw. This inspired him to invent the cloud chamber, which was of prime importance in particle physics research for many years. He was awarded the Nobel Prize for Physics in 1927, and died in Carlops in 1959.

Keep on the path until you join the road. Turn right here, then after about 100m left at a wooden gate with a sign next to it indicating Scald Law. Go along the track (ignoring the gate and bridge leading off to the left for Turnhouse Hill).

Bothy at Glencorse

2 Go through two more self-closing gates and carry on until you reach a circular stone building and a slate-roofed stone bothy. These buildings and the disused filter beds adjacent to them are part of the water supply system from Glencorse Reservoir.

The Ordnance Survey map of 1852 names Glencorse Reservoir and the neighbourhood 'Glencross'. The stone bothy has the date 1901 on its chimney, and was probably built as a tool store for the water keeper. The **filter beds** opposite were part of the water purification system, and consisted of layers of clean sand where the raw water was run through to trap dirt and sediment. The sand would require replacing regularly, a task that was done manually by digging out the old sand with spades and shovels.

Walk past the three filter beds in this sheltered valley. Go on up the track to a white wooden gate with a self-closing gate to the left. Go through the gate and turn out onto the road.

A green woodpecker is often heard calling in the **valley where the filter beds** are located, and the rooks in the plantation further up the track make a cacophony in spring. The rook can be identified from its cousin the carrion crow by the whitish patch at the base of its bill. This area is good for bats, and the Ranger Service has put up both wooden and 'woodcrete' bat boxes to provide roost sites for pipistrelles.

3 Turn left and walk up **Flotterstone Glen road**, passing lovely **Glen Cottage** and **Glencorse Reservoir** on your left. The clump of Scots pines growing on the island on Glencorse Reservoir lends to the Highland atmosphere. There are also likely to be cormorants and feral greylag geese here. Continue along the road until you come to a wooden gate on your right, set slightly above the road, with a signpost indicating Castlelaw.

Walk up the rough path by the conifer plantation until you reach a kissing gate and another signpost. Go through the gate and turn left and walk northwest on a good stony track. Live firing ranges are situated in the hillside to your right. Do not enter this area when the red flags are flying or the lamps are lit. The track contours round **Castlelaw Hill**. Stop to enjoy the view over **Turnhouse Hill** and Glencorse Reservoir to the southwest.

4 Stay on the track, passing former quarries and pits as the path turns north and becomes parallel to **Kirk Burn**, down to the left. Walk up this sheltered glen, over some boggy ground, for a further kilometre until you join the track leading from Castlelaw to Dreghorn. Just to the right of the track, at NT223656, there is a square, flat stone amongst the grass. This is a boundary stone that marked the boundary between Glencorse and Colinton parishes.

5 Turn right on the Castlelaw–Dreghorn track, going up over the small hillock of **Fala Knowe**.

A few metres off the track to the right, at NT226653, a spring rises that flows in to Kirk Burn. This is known as the **Colonel's Well**. William Anderson refers to the well in *The Pentland Hills* (see bibliography), and remarks at the water's delicious taste and coolness, in addition to its reliability even in dry summers, the exception being 1911. The well still has its stone trough, but is quite overgrown and weed covered, and not appetising in the least.

Continue on the track from the Colonel's Well for a further 500m until you reach a stony track to your right.

6 The stony track leads to the summit of **Castlelaw Hill** at 488m, and from here the Army flies a red flag when the firing ranges are in use. The view from the top is good, taking in the Moorfoots, Lammermuirs and Border hills, as well as the rest of the Pentlands and further afield to the Ochils.

Either descend by the same track, or walk east down through the heather, staying to the left (north) of the fence marking the danger area, to reach the main track.

7 At the track turn right and walk south towards **Castlelaw** farm, stopping on the rise above the Iron Age fort and souterrain to look at the ditches and ramparts on the hillside. The fort and souterrain are in the care of Historic Scotland, which has provided two information boards about the site and its history. Continue downhill towards the farm, going through a kissing gate to reach Castlelaw car park, then taking a narrow path where there is a signpost indicating Glencorse Reservoir and Flotterstone.

The path skirts around the wall of a farmhouse, now used as a training centre for the Territorial Army, and comes out by a large shed. From here go left along a wide track, passing a conifer plantation on the left and an army building on the right. Opposite the army building is a path signposted to Flotterstone, which winds its way down to Flotterstone Glen road.

At the kissing gate at the bottom turn left and walk down the road to your starting point at Flotterstone car park.

WALK 24
Two Cleuchs

Distance	18km
Ascent	195m
Time	4 hours 50 minutes
Maps	Ordnance Survey Landranger 66
	Ordnance Survey Explorer 344
Start/Finish	Flotterstone car park NT232631

This is an easy walk, with the first 6km on a tarmac road, making the countryside easily accessible for people of many abilities. The views are good and there is a variety of landscapes to enjoy. This is probably one of the most popular walks in the Pentlands, and part of the route can be enjoyed by families with young children.

1 The route starts at **Flotterstone** car park, at NT232631, which may be busy at weekends and holidays. From the car park take a good path that leads through woodland and heads west, passing the blue plaque to CTR Wilson, the eminent physicist who was born near here at Crosshouse Farm (see Walk 23 for further information).

Turn left where the path joins **Flotterstone Glen road** and continue up the road past the picnic site at **Buckie Brae**, on your right.

2 Walk up the road past Glen Cottage, which is next to **Glencorse Reservoir**.

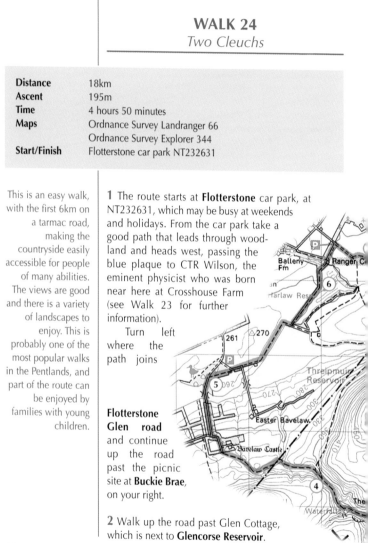

Glencorse Reservoir was constructed between 1819 and 1822. The dam caused difficulties, because of the enormous quantity of gravel (53 feet or 16m in depth) that had to be excavated to reach solid rock. There are two tunnels in the embankment, one for supply, the other a safety tunnel to let out surplus water. The release of this water forms two lovely cascades in the glen below the dam. The reservoir was designed by the great Scottish civil engineer Thomas Telford, and the work was supervised by James Jardine. The construction employed 300 men for three years and cost £209,000.

Walk along the road overlooking the reservoir, past a small pine-clad island that is linked to the shore by a stone causeway. There are lovely views to

Turnhouse and **Carnethy** from here. Continue on and cross a small stone bridge that spans **Kirk Burn** as it flows down from between **Capelaw Hill** and **Castlelaw Hill**.

Glen Road and Turnhouse Hill

From the bridge over Kirk Burn, about 20m out into the reservoir, lie the submerged ruins of the chapel of **St Katherine's in the Hopes**. The founding of the chapel is connected with the story (perhaps apocryphal) of a royal deer hunt. According to the story, King Robert the Bruce staked the Pentland estate against the life of Sir William Saint Clair, with the outcome of the hunt of a white deer by the knight and his two hounds, 'Help' and 'Hold', being the deciding factor. Fortunately the dogs managed to bring down the deer, and in gratitude, and to mark the spot, Sir William had a chapel built in the valley. The full story, and a photograph of the ruins, are in *Pentland Days and Country Ways* by Will Grant. Place names nearby also reflect past events, with Knightfield Rig, King's Hill and Kirkton Farm found here.

Keep on the road, passing an area of open marsh known as **Double Waters** (there is often a grey heron standing patiently by the water's edge). Pass by **Logan Cottage** and **Logan House**, with Logan Burn tucked down below the level of the road. Logan Burn is a good spot for grey wagtails and dippers.

3 The road climbs slightly and then the embankment of **Loganlea Reservoir** is reached. Walk along to the end of the road, where it then becomes a good path, passing the former shepherd's house at **The Howe**, and then crossing a bridge where there is a signpost.

> **Loganlea Reservoir** was constructed between 1847 and 1851 by the Edinburgh Water Company, following a succession of dry summers and an increased demand for water from Edinburgh's New Town. About 500m beyond the dam, where a small burn enters the reservoir from the north, there are the remains of a house called the Howlet's House ('owl's house'), perhaps the priest's house for St Katherine's Chapel, or a hospice or inn for drovers travelling to the sheep and cattle markets at House o' Muir (see Walk 22).

4 Follow the signpost indicating Balerno as it points towards **Green Cleuch**. Keep to the left side of the burn on a path until you cross the burn by a wooden footbridge. ▶ Walk through the steep-sided cleuch, the pink felsite rocks of the scree slopes of **Black Hill** forming a rocky path. The path cuts through the glen for approximately 2km before opening out to more open, grassy ground by **Bavelaw Castle**, at NT166626.

From here climb a stile next to a gate, and walk down a rough track until it joins a metalled road that forms the entrance to Bavelaw Castle, a private residence, on the right. Continue straight down this road as it bends to the left, and then at a junction at the top of a steep hill, turn right down the hill between two lines of beech trees.

5 At the bottom of the hill, cross **Threipmuir Reservoir** at **Redford Bridge**.

> **Redford Bridge** is an excellent vantage point from which to watch water birds such as black-headed gulls, moorhens, teal, mallard and little grebe. The fortunes of the black-headed gull have waxed and

The fenced enclosure around the waterfall to your left is to protect the rare and unusual lime-loving plants found here. The site was designated a SSSI in 1985 (see also Walk 8).

Threipmuir Reservoir from Redford Bridge

waned, largely due to water-level changes and weather conditions. In *The Birds of the Pentland Hills* I Munro gives a detailed chronicle of the species. The gulls' eggs were once collected as a substitute for the more valuable peewits' eggs, because to uninitiated Edwardian gourmets, they look very similar. This western end of the reservoir, called Bavelaw Marsh, is a SSSI because of its birds and plant life. If you have time, it is worth visiting the bird hide located on the south side of the reservoir. It can be easily reached by re-tracing your steps back over the bridge and going through a metal gate to pick up a narrow grassy path. The path runs between the iron fencing at the bottom of the fields and the scrubby willows and alders that fringe Threipmuir Reservoir. The hide is an ideal vantage point from which to observe some of the wildlife in the area without causing disturbance. There is good information about what can be seen and heard according to the season.

From the hide, return to the road and cross Redford Bridge.

From Redford Bridge continue along the metalled road, with **Red Moss** to your left and woodland to your right. Opposite the start of the Red Moss Nature Reserve boardwalk there is a path and an interpretation board on the right. Take this path as it skirts the edge of Redford Wood, which is semi-natural birch woodland.

The path emerges at a stony track that heads towards Threipmuir Reservoir, signposted to Harlaw. Walk to the right along the track, passing a small conifer plantation to the right. Go through a gate, going down gradually towards a fishing hut near the reservoir. Keep on the track as it goes along the northwestern shore of Threipmuir Reservoir until you reach the dam and spillway. At this point keep left by the spillway and follow a signpost indicating Harlaw Ranger Centre.

6 Walk along the track on the north side of **Harlaw Reservoir** to the Ranger Centre at **Harlaw House**, the former water-keeper's house. (The building is open daily except Christmas Day and New Year's Day, and has leaflets, displays and information as well as a toilet. For opening hours contact the Pentland Hills Ranger Service on 0131 445 3383.) Go along the metalled road that leads back towards Harlaw car park.

7 At Harlaw car park turn right onto a good track that leads south towards **Maiden's Cleuch**. After about 300m the track divides and you should follow the left fork, signposted to Glencorse. Go through a couple of self-closing bridle gates (this route is popular with horses and mountain bikers) before reaching the stone stile at the top of the cleuch.

Go over the stile and enjoy the unfolding view down towards **Glencorse Reservoir**. From the stile just keep on the path until you come to a gate leading out onto Flotterstone Glen road. Turn left and make your way back to the car park via the road.

WALK 25
Pentland Tops

Distance	21km
Ascent	1210m
Time	7 hours 15 minutes
Maps	Ordnance Survey Landranger 66
	Ordnance Survey Explorer 344
Start/Finish	Flotterstone car park NT232631

This walk takes in a good number of the main summits in the northern area of the Pentlands and, at 21km and 1210m of ascent, makes for a good hill day. You may of course curtail the route at a number of places, depending on time and circumstances.

1 Begin the walk at **Flotterstone**. There is a car park at NT232631, although this does become very busy at weekends, so either arrive early, or travel by bus or cycle. Leave the car park and walk west on a good path through some woodland, passing the CTR Wilson blue plaque (see Walk 23) and joining **Flotterstone Glen road**.

Turn right onto the road and after about 100m, at a signpost indicating Scald Law, turn left through a wooden gate and walk along a rough track to a gate where there is another signpost indicating Scald Law.

2 Cross the wooden bridge a few metres from the signpost and head uphill on a path over two grassy and bracken-covered ridges before

the long pull uphill on **Turnhouse Hill**. Route
finding is not a problem here, as
there is a good path leading
up to the summit, which is
marked by a cairn.

3 Head off on
the   path
south-
west

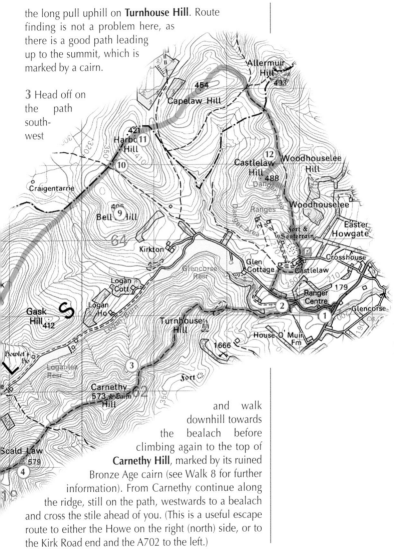

and   walk
downhill towards
the   bealach   before
climbing again to the top of
Carnethy Hill, marked by its ruined
Bronze Age cairn (see Walk 8 for further
information). From Carnethy continue along
the ridge, still on the path, westwards to a bealach
and cross the stile ahead of you. (This is a useful escape
route to either the Howe on the right (north) side, or to
the Kirk Road end and the A702 to the left.)

The ridge from Hare Hill

4 From the bealach climb **Scald Law** by the stony zigzag path that winds its way up to the trig point on the summit. Again continue westwards, still on the path, with the option of diverting to visit **South Black Hill**. (This diversion is not shown on the map, but the route description is as follows. Walk about 200m from the summit of Scald Law, then detour left on a peaty path to the cairn on top of the hill. Walk back along the same path, then veer left to rejoin the main path from Scald Law to East Kip.)

5 Ascend **East Kip** and **West Kip** in quick succession. There is an obvious path over the tops of these two hills, which are about 700m apart.

6 Descend **West Kip** quite steeply down to a good path, and turn right (north) on a gentle slope to cross **Logan Burn** (follow the signpost to Balerno at the path junction).

7 Keep on this path for another 500m. At a wooden post, 200m before a metal gate in the dyke, take an ATV track right for 100m before walking up another ATV track to the summit of Hare Hill, marked by three small cairns and a disused quarry.

Come off Hare Hill on the same ATV track, to join another ATV track. At this track turn left and follow it until it reaches a fence. Stay on this track as it goes down to join a path in Green Cleuch.

8 Turn left and walk along through the cleuch until you come to a narrow path by a gate in the dyke, climbing up to the right through the heather on the side of **Black Hill**. Go up the path next to the drystane dyke to the top of the rise.

From the top of the rise walk alongside the dyke for about 100m to locate an ATV track climbing steeply through the heather to reach the flattish summit of Black Hill (501m). From the top of Black Hill walk straight ahead (northeast) on an ATV track to gradually descend down over the heather to Dens Cleuch. The ATV track narrows to a path that follows a line of wooden shooting butts – keep on this.

The name Dens Cleuch is recorded on Knox's map of 1812, and originates from *dens*, referring to the deep gullies in the watershed of the pass; 'cleuch' is from Middle English *cloghe*, a ravine. The ground here is very wet, even in summer, and parts of the cleuch are a raised peat bog with rare plants. Take extreme care crossing this area, and avoid damaging the fragile habitat of the bog.

9 Climb steeply out of Dens Cleuch on a path that veers to the left by the fence and dyke. Ascend the side of **Bell's Hill** before dropping down to Maiden's Cleuch, as follows. There is a drystane dyke about 500m to the left (north) of the summit of Bell's Hill. Walk down to this dyke and keep it on your left down to Maiden's Cleuch. ▶

There is a good view across to Glencorse Reservoir from the hillside here.

The marshy areas next to the path are where a small plant called **hairy stonecrop** grows. It is a low-growing (15cm) plant with five pink petals and sticky glands on its leaves. It grows in mountainous areas in rocky but wet places. This is one of the few sites in Midlothian where the plant is found, and the Ranger Service counts the number of plants each year to monitor the population.

10 From the stone stile at Maiden's Cleuch go through a gate to the right (ignore the gate to the left of the stone stile) and take the path up the grassy slope of **Harbour Hill** (421m). Keeping to the path on the right (south) side of the fence and drystane dyke. The top can be boggy in places, but the going is very easy.

11 From the top of Harbour Hill take the path down into Phantom's Cleuch (see Walk 5), then on a grassy path to your right ascend the rounded lump of **Capelaw Hill** (454m). Walk over the flat plateau of the hill and descend off the east side to a gate and a cattle-grid in a drystane dyke with a stile to the right of it. Go over the stile and up a narrow path through the heather to join a wider stony track.

12 Turn right along the track and walk up over the hillock of **Fala Knowe**, and after about 500m bear right up a stony path that winds up the north side of **Castlelaw Hill**, to the summit beacon at 468m.

Return to the main track, either by a direct descent east to the left of the fence through the heather, or by the outward route. From here take the track down towards **Castlelaw** farm.

The lines of the ramparts of the **hill fort** are best viewed from this track, as the outline of the prehistoric structure can be appreciated from a short distance away. A detour into the souterrain gives a good impression of how the area was used by the early peoples of the Pentlands.

Walk down to the farm, passing through the car park where a signpost indicates Glencorse Reservoir and Flotterstone. Make for a wooden gate to the right of a

barn, and a narrow path that skirts the wall around the farm buildings (the former farmhouse is used by the army as a training base). The path emerges by a large shed and a track continues around the perimeter of the farm and firing ranges.

Ridge and Glencorse Reservoir

To return to Flotterstone, follow the track until you go through a kissing gate near a building whose window shutters are painted in a camouflage pattern. Here there is a signpost to the left indicating Flotterstone, and you should follow the stony path down through the gorse to Flotterstone Glen road. At the kissing gate turn left and walk down the road back to the start point at the car park.

WALK 26
Historical Hike

Distance	8km
Ascent	490m
Time	2 hours 50 minutes
Maps	Ordnance Survey Landranger 66
	Ordnance Survey Explorer 344
Start/Finish	Castlelaw Farm NT229637

This walk offers views over Midlothian and then across the city and beyond. There is a good sprinkling of prehistoric and historic sites, as well as open hill and wooded landscapes.

1 This is a good alternative to the madding crowds at Flotterstone, especially on a sunny Sunday where parking can be a challenge. There are limited spaces at **Castlelaw** farm, but not usually any difficulty finding a spot. This is a working sheep farm, and the area is used by the army for live firing on the ranges and for other training across their ground, so please access the route responsibly.

From the car park at NT229637 go through the wooden kissing gate (there is a signpost indicating Dreghorn 3M to guide you) and head up a stony path northwards towards the souterrain and hill fort. Detour into the souterrain and over the ditches of the hill fort. Interpretation boards provided by Historic Scotland explain the history of the site (see also Walk 5).

2 Return to the main track and begin an easy and gradual ascent that skirts to the east of **Castlelaw Hill**. (A climb to the summit at 488m can be made by leaving the track at NT228649 and taking the stony path to the top. This adds about 1km to the walk.)

3 Back on the main track, go over the small rise at **Fala Knowe**. The view back across the Pentland ridge is excellent from here. Continue until you come to a cattle-grid, and at this point veer right on a muddy path that hugs a fence.

> **Skylarks** can often be heard at Fala Knowe. The skylark, or 'laverock' as it is called locally, was once eaten as a delicacy by the Victorians. A celebratory dinner for the opening of the Forth Railway Bridge in 1890 included a huge pie of 300 skylarks. Thankfully those days are over, and the skylark can sing unhindered.

4 The path climbs gradually at first, then more steeply towards the summit of **Allermuir Hill**, with its trig point and viewpoint indicator, gifted by the Russell family in 1963 (see Walk 1). Having enjoyed the views (on a clear day) descend on a stepped path, keeping the fence line close to your right.

Go over another small rise on the same path before reaching an obvious bealach below **Caerketton Hill** at NT232662, where there is a wooden stile. ▶ Climb the stile and head down a grassy slope to another stile in an area called Windy Door Nick (where it is always either very windy, hence the name, or extremely tranquil).

On the slope here there are a good number of healthy, if windswept, juniper bushes (see Walk 1).

> At **Windy Door Nick** you may see, or more likely hear, red grouse – they nest in the heather on the slopes of Woodhouselee Hill. There are also wheatears around

Boghall masts

in the summer, arriving around the last week of March (although climate change may make a difference to arrival and departure dates for migrating birds).

5 Over the stile, follow the path for about 1.5km as it cuts south down **Boghall Glen**, crossing a number of stiles on the way, making for **Boghall Farm**.

On the shoulder of Caerketton Hill there are two **tall wooden masts** connected by a number of wires. These are the remains of a high frequency radio aerial, erected during the Second World War to receive signals from South Africa. There are also some telegraph poles that carried wires from the aerial to a small building near the farm.

Pass the **Second World War masts**, and 200m downhill, at a clump of larch and Scots pines, go through a kissing gate where there is a sign marked 'car park'. Walk down beside a fence to another kissing gate next to a former shepherd's cottage. Go through the kissing gate and continue for a few metres past the cottage until you see a set of worn wooden steps on your right, leading down the slope into the little glen where **Boghall Burn** flows. Go down the steps, cross the burn by a wooden footbridge, then ascend the steps up the slope on the other side.

These fields are important lambing fields and responsible access to avoid disturbing stock and damaging fences or gates should be taken.

6 At the top of the steps, still on the path, go right and cross a fence. Walk up the slope along the right-hand edge of the field to the trees further up on the lower slopes of **Woodhouselee Hill**. ◄

When you reach the lower edge of the trees go left, following the field edge, which is fenced up to your right. Keep on the edge of the trees until you reach another fence running downhill. Go over this fence and keep straight on to cross a muddy ditch. You will reach a point where four fences meet – cross the two upper fences on your right. Walk straight ahead beside another fence, which you should keep on your left. Walk to the end of this fence to a small building, and at the building take a path up to the right alongside a fence.

Go along the fence until you reach a fairly wobbly stile and cross the fence at NT235645, just before a cattle-grid. Go down through the trees and shrubs to cross a burn, then climb the slope on the other side. Just beyond the burn cross the fence to your right.

7 To your left are a muddy path and a fenced corridor. Walk up here for about 300m until you come to a large sandstone obelisk on your left, over 6m in height and in the shape of a Celtic cross.

Fraser Tytler monument

The magnificent Celtic cross monument was erected in 1893 by the Fraser Tytler family of **Woodhouselee**, and commemorates William Tytler, Alexander Fraser Tytler and James Tytler, all interred in Greyfriars kirkyard. There is much folklore and legend about this area. The original castle of Woodhouselee stood on the banks of the River Esk near Auchendinny. Stones and timber from the old castle were brought to Fulford to construct a new residence, possibly in the 16th century, although the dates are unknown. It was said that ghosts were imported with the old stones, a tale that Walter Scott, a frequent visitor to Woodhouselee, helped to perpetuate. Scott was a guest of the literary Tytler family who owned the house from 1748 to 1923.

8 From the memorial, keep on the path as it meanders through some old Scots pine trees to just below **Castle Knowe**. Walk on a grassy path alongside the drystane dyke and return to the start at Castlelaw Farm.

View from Castle Knowe

WALK 27
Exploring Caerketton

Distance	5km
Ascent	283m
Time	1hour 45 minutes
Maps	Ordnance Survey Landranger 66
	Ordnance Survey Explorer 344
Start/Finish	Boghall Farm car park NT245652

1 Begin from the car park at **Boghall Farm** NT245652. Go out of a wooden gate at the rear of the car park and head uphill through a fenced corridor that skirts the periphery of the farm buildings. (At the gate leading to the fenced corridor there is a signpost indicating Boghall Glen, Hillend and Swanston, as well as a post with information about Pentland Hills Produce.)

This is a lovely round if you are short of time and don't want parking difficulties or crowds. Naturally the views are fine, and the mixed habitats and relative peace and quiet mean there is a good chance of seeing wildlife.

Boghall Farm is owned by the Scottish Agricultural College. It was purchased in 1922 as an experimental farm by the then Edinburgh and East of Scotland College of Agriculture. Besides its use for crop trials and plant breeding, the farm is visited by students learning about agriculture and land management. The activities at Boghall reflect changes

Boghall Burn

in farming, and the large-scale potato trial plots, piggery or hen houses are no longer here. The *Scotsman* newspaper reports that in October 1933, 25 unemployed men from Edinburgh visited Boghall to learn about pig and poultry rearing, so agriculture for the wider community was on the agenda 70 years ago.

From the Boghall Glen/Hillend/Swanston signpost the fenced corridor leads to another track that goes left uphill again to a former shepherd's cottage. Next to the cottage is a kissing gate that leads into a field. After a short walk uphill alongside a fence and some sheep buchts (pens), there is another kissing gate and a sign indicating Boghall Glen, Hillend and Swanston. Follow the finger pointing to Boghall Glen.

Go through the scrubby pine and larch plantation to head diagonally left (northwest) to pick up a track that climbs gradually through rough pasture fields. Take the track as it heads right up **Boghall Glen**, staying parallel to **Boghall Burn**, which flows from the numerous springs that rise on the slopes of **Caerketton Hill**. Continue on the track, crossing three stiles. The going is good, although the upper parts of the route may be muddy and churned up by stock. ◄

There are sheep and sometimes suckler beef cows and calves in these fields, so please take care and access the area responsibly if you have a dog.

The slopes of **Caerketton Hill**, and also **Woodhouselee Hill**, are good places to see buzzards and kestrels, as well as red grouse on the heathery margins. Buzzards have staged a real comeback over the past decade, with numbers rising. Ian Munro, in his 1988 book *The Birds of the Pentland Hills* (see bibliography), records the buzzard as an 'occasional visitor' – now they are often referred to as 'the tourists' eagle', and although considerably smaller than the golden eagle, still a joy to watch. The nest and home range are defended fiercely – as I know, after being swooped upon by a protective bird while out running in the hills.

After climbing the third stile the track becomes a path as it narrows through the heather, and you eventually reach another stile at the bottom of a short, steep grassy slope at aptly named Windy Door Nick. This is a spot where it is always either blowing a gale, or an oasis of stillness and tranquillity. Walk on the path up this slope to arrive at yet another stile.

2 Climb the stile, walk a few metres straight ahead and turn right onto a path that goes up in a westerly direction onto the stony slopes of Caerketton Hill. ▶ Climb steeply up the hill, and enjoy the great views over Edinburgh and beyond, unfolding below as you walk along almost a kilometre of fine ridge.

There are a good few juniper bushes here, protected from sheep grazing. W Anderson (see bibliography) remarks on the bushes, but complains that the fruits are dry as dust.

The **cairn** close to the summit of Caerketton Hill is a Scheduled Ancient Monument. The place name Caerketton is recorded on Adair's map of 1682 as 'Kairnketton' and on later maps as 'Kirkyetten' (1763), 'Kirketton' (1773), 'Kirkyetton' (1817) and 'Caerketton' (1852). In *The Place Names of Edinburgh*, S Harris suggests the name is British, from *carn*, meaning 'rocky summit', *caid*, meaning a burial cairn, and the suffix *an*, meaning 'place of', the result being 'rocky summit at the burial cairn place'.

Walking along Caerketton ridge

At the eastern end of the ridge the path descends steeply and zigzags down to a fence, signpost and stile. Cross the stile.

> Just over the stile a grassy knoll marks the site of an **Iron Age hill fort**. There is little evidence of it today, except some grassy ramparts and ditches, although the site is a Scheduled Ancient Monument.

3 At the stile follow the sign indicating Boghall and head downhill, almost south, keeping the fence and ruined drystane dyke to your right as you wind through gorse scrub, until you reach the trees at the bottom and a stile. ◄

This is a good spot to hear or see the green woodpecker. At the bottom of the path there is another signpost indicating Boghall.

4 Climb the stile that crosses the fence, and then immediately pick up a narrow path that follows the upper areas of **Boghall Plantation**, skirting the lower easterly slopes of Caerketton Hill. Parts of the path may be muddy, and sometimes overgrown, but it is otherwise good walking.

> **Buzzards** and **roe deer** can sometimes be seen around this area. Less likely is a sighting of a little auk (a small seabird about half the size of a puffin), which was found by Mr Wilson, the farm manager at the time, on his driveway at Boghall in February 1940, after some northeast gales.

The yellow, coconut-scented gorse flowers give out a fantastic bouquet on a warm summer's day, and it is worth pausing to inhale deeply.

The path hugs the tree line for about 500m, then you pass into a corridor of gorse. ◄ The path comes out of the gorse by the Second World War radio masts (see Walk 26), and a stile crosses the fence just above the masts.

From the stile descend the slope to the conifer plantation, go through the kissing gate and cross the field down to the former shepherd's cottage. From the cottage retrace your steps, picking up the track that leads down to the farm. Go through the wooden gate to the left that goes back to the start point at the car park.

WALK 28
Find Your Way

Distance	8km
Ascent	390m
Time	2 hours 40 minutes
Maps	Ordnance Survey Landranger 66
	Ordnance Survey Explorer 344
Start/Finish	Boghall Farm car park NT245652

1 The walk begins at **Boghall Farm** car park at NT245652. There is a small parking area that rarely becomes full, even at weekends.

Go through a gate at the rear of the car park and head uphill, going through another gate between two fences as they skirt the boundary of the farm buildings. At the start of the fenced corridor there is a signpost

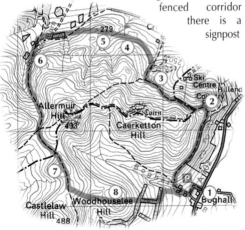

This is a personal favourite, and a route I sometimes use when leading map and compass courses. It is good from a navigational point of view because it has a rich variety of landforms to identify, as well as some featureless broken ground to practise micro-navigation.
It also has lots of interesting cultural and natural heritage, and lovely views.

151

Boghall Glen

indicating Boghall Glen, Hillend and Swanston. Follow the signpost as you walk through the fenced corridor until you reach a gate at the back of the farm.

Go through this gate, turn right and take the stony track leading uphill (northwest) to a former shepherd's cottage. To the right of the cottage are a field gate and a kissing gate. Go through the kissing gate and uphill along the edge of the field by some sheep buchts (pens) for about 100m to another kissing gate near some pine and larch trees (there is a signpost here indicating Hillend).

Go through the kissing gate, and keeping the fence on your right, walk uphill steeply towards two large wooden masts that were once part of a high-frequency radio aerial. Just beyond the masts is a stile that crosses the fence. Climb over here to pick up a path that goes into thick gorse and along the top edge of Boghall Plantation. Follow this path for about 700m to another signpost indicating Swanston, next to a stile.

Cross the fence by the stile and climb a grassy path, rising away steeply to the left alongside a fence and tumbled-down drystane dyke.

2 At the top of the hill cross the fence by a stile and walk right (northwest) above the ski tows and chairlift of the snow sports centre. There is also a signpost indicating

Swanston here, by the stile. You will pass three wooden fenced enclosures containing juniper bushes (see Walk 1). The views over the city are excellent on a clear day.

3 Keep on the path as it goes down the northern slopes of **Caerketton Hill** towards the **T Wood** and Lothianburn Golf Course. At a SRWS signpost ignore the indicators for both Swanston and Allermuir and take a path that goes to the left of the path to Swanston, north of **Muilieputchie** (see Walk 2 and shown on OS 344), and follows the line of a ruined drystane dyke. Keep to this path, with the dyke to your left.

4 The ground is quite undulating and featureless, and ideal for practising navigation skills. Keep on the path as it goes downhill.

To the north the rocky outcrops above Swanston Golf Course are called **Stotfold Craigs**. According to S Harris (see bibliography) this may be Stodfauld Craigs, which is Scots for 'crags above the stodfauld'. The word *stot* meant a bullock in later Scots, although in early use it meant horse or bull. *Fauld* was a fold or enclosure.

This area was probably well-known to the young **Robert Louis Stevenson**, whose family had the summer tenancy on Swanston Cottage, the large white house that can be seen nestling below Torgeith Knowe to the west of Swanston Farm. The young man wandered around the hillside, making bad verse and tagging along with John Tod, the 'Roarin' Shepherd', and others.

Keep on the path as it crosses **Hare Burn**. From Hare Burn there are two prominent knolls ahead. On a path, go uphill between **Todhole Knowe** and **Shearie Knowe**. (On OS 66, go to the left of spot height 279m.)

According to Stuart Harris (see bibliography) the 'Shearie' part may be derived from Celtic, containing *siar*, meaning 'west', or even *sear*, meaning 'dark' or 'black', and could refer to either a hill or a burn. Todhole Knowe is simpler, meaning 'knowe with/near the fox's den'.

5 On reaching the ground between the knolls you will be faced with a fence. Walk alongside the fence and cross it before it turns at right angles. Maintain height as you contour round the hill on a path and cross the small burns that flow down into **Smithy Cleuch**. Again contour round the hill on a path, but descend below the rocky cliffs marked as **Green Craig** on Ordnance Survey Explorer 344, at NT222669. In a cleft in these rocks a hoard of bones was found, including those of reindeer, hence the name **Reindeer Cave** (see Walk 2).

6 Keep on the path then join the track as it ascends **Howden Glen**. It is a gradual pull, and relentless if running or biking – the track is known to some as 'the elevator' for its apparently interminable nature. The climb does end though, and levels off at a crossroads of paths – to the right (west) over Capelaw Hill, the left (east) to Allermuir Hill, behind (south) to Dreghorn, and our route straight ahead (north) to **Fala Knowe**. Walk along the track, crossing a cattle-grid, although there is a stile to the right of the grid.

7 There are two potential short diversions from the cattle-grid. The first is to locate the small, flat, square **boundary stone**, marked 'BS', at NT223656. This is a fun challenge for participants on map and compass courses, who by this stage are supremely confident of their map-reading and micro-navigation skills.

From the cattle-grid on the main route walk over the rise at Fala Knowe, about 200m further along, and on to the low point between Fala Knowe and another slight rise. From this point you may wish to locate the **Colonel's Well**, marked 'W', at NT226653. (Descriptions of the boundary stone and the Colonel's Well are given in Walk 23.)

At this low point on the track (NT228654) leave the track and walk to the left (due east) down **Woodhouselee Hill**. ▶ The ground is quite rough and heathery, but there are sheep tracks through the heather that make walking easier.

8 Walk over Woodhouselee Hill and down to a line of shelter belts on the east side of the hill (from the track to the shelter belts is about 1km). At the shelter belts there is a fence – cross this using a gate, then make your way across a field to another shelter belt. At the second shelter belt cross another fence using a gate and walk across another field, aiming for the left-hand corner downhill. There are gates on the way, and it is possible to use field margins to avoid disturbing stock.

Cross a fence above Boghall Farm and follow a narrow path. This joins a wider path where you turn left down a set of steps, crossing **Boghall Burn** by a wooden footbridge. At the footbridge climb up some more steps, and at the top turn right and walk along the track towards the farm.

The track rejoins the outward route at the fenced corridor through a gate to the left behind the farm and returns to the car park at the start.

This area is used for sheep grazing, so exercise your access responsibly and minimise disturbance.

View south up Howden Glen

155

WALK 29
Reservoir Round

Distance	20km
Ascent	275m
Time	5 hours 30 minutes
Maps	Ordnance Survey Landranger 66
	Ordnance Survey Explorer 344
Start/Finish	Bonaly car park NT211675

This route passes seven of the reservoirs in the Pentland Hills. Although Bonaly is suggested as a start point, the walk can begin from Flotterstone, Harlaw or Threipmuir car parks as alternatives. The advantage of starting from Bonaly is that you get the height gain at the start of the walk, while you are still fresh, and thereafter there are only easy, gradual ascents, and you can relax and enjoy the scenery.

1 Begin from **Bonaly car park**, beyond the scout camp at NT211675. From the car park go through the gate and climb steeply up the track as it heads into the trees. Continue along the track until you come to another gate. Go through this gate and out onto heather moorland, still on the track.

2 Keep on the track for a further 800m before going through a gate that goes into the fenced area of **Bonaly Reservoir**.

Bonaly Reservoir is the oldest in the Pentland Hills, constructed in 1851. Two earlier smaller 'ponds' were built in 1789. Evidence of the old embankment can be seen on your left just after the gate at NT212663. When the reservoir was drained for repairs to the tower in 1998 a number of Victorian bottles and clay smoking pipes were found in the silt. These probably belonged to the workers who dug out the reservoir.

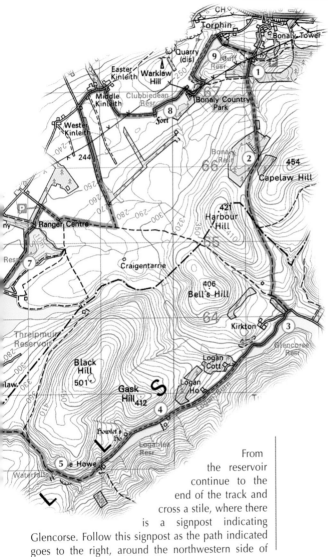

From the reservoir continue to the end of the track and cross a stile, where there is a signpost indicating Glencorse. Follow this signpost as the path indicated goes to the right, around the northwestern side of

Capelaw Hill, to reach the path through **Phantom's Cleuch**. The path crosses a small tributary of **Kirk Burn** by a wooden bridge, then drops south over **Knightfield Rig** to reach **Glencorse Reservoir** at the wooden gate leading onto the **Glen Road** (NT216640).

3 At the gate there is a sign indicating Loganlea Reservoir 1.5M. Turn right and head along the road beside Glencorse Reservoir. Keep on the road as it passes the western end of Glencorse. **Logan Burn**, close to the road on your left, forms the linking watercourse between Loganlea and Glencorse reservoirs.

> **Logan Burn** is a good spot for the grey heron and the common sandpiper, as well as the superbly adapted dipper or water ouzel. The dipper has specially modified dense bones to counteract buoyancy, and its wings form small hydroplanes to help it move underwater. It feeds on small insects and larvae.

Just behind the office a rough track leads up to ruined Howlet's House (see Walk 24). It is worth the short diversion up the track for the view over Loganlea towards Carnethy Hill.

4 Follow the tarmac road alongside Logan Burn for approximately 1km until you pass the former water-keeper's house and reach **Loganlea Reservoir**. After another 500m there is an office for the trout fishery on the right. ◄

Glencorse and Bell's Hill

Back on the main route, continue along the road to where it becomes a track, just by **The Howe**. The Howe was once the residence of the local shepherd, and was a single-storey dwelling.

Looking over Threipmuir Reservoir (PHRS)

5 Pass by the Howe and keep to the path on the left of the burn until you reach a wooden bridge. Cross Logan Burn, heading through narrow **Green Cleuch**, between **Black Hill** and **Hare Hill**. The fenced area around the waterfall is a SSSI, because of its rare plants. Keep on the stony path as it winds northwest. There are a couple of stiles to negotiate on the way, but it is a pleasant walk that eventually opens out at a grassy sward.

Follow the path across the grassy area, heading for a gate and a stile by the boundary wall to **Bavelaw Castle**. Go over the stile and walk down a rough track that becomes a tarmac road. Pass the entrance to the castle on your right and go down the road until you reach a junction at the top of a steep hill, lined with beech trees. Walk straight down the beech avenue, enjoying the wildlife here – usually birds. ▶

Along the beech avenue there are willow warblers and chiff chaff in summer, as well as buzzards and lapwings, and also fungi and mosses, depending on the season.

159

6 At the bottom of the hill **Redford Bridge** crosses **Threipmuir Reservoir**, the fourth of the round.

> **Threipmuir Reservoir**, along with **Harlaw** and **Harperrig**, supply compensation flow to the Water of Leith. These three reservoirs were constructed to ensure a steady and reliable supply of water to the numerous mills along the river. Products such as grain, snuff, flax and paper were produced, and cloth was waulked (thrashed) and animal hides tanned. (A good walk that could be joined to one of the Pentlands routes would be along the length of the Water of Leith walkway, from Balerno to Leith.)

After Redford Bridge walk straight along the road, passing Redford Stables, partially obscured by trees on the right, and **Red Moss Nature Reserve** to the left. Just opposite the entrance to the nature reserve is a large information board highlighting some of the special wildlife in this area. A signpost next to the board points the way to Harlaw.

Take the narrow path that skirts the southern edge of **Redford Wood**. The path emerges at another track, where there is a further signpost indicating Harlaw. Follow the wide track as it passes a conifer plantation to the right. At the end of the trees go straight on through a gate and head down the track towards the main body of Threipmuir Reservoir. There is a small fishing hut on the right, and two more gates to negotiate before you reach the shore of the reservoir proper. ◄

The water is a good place to see gulls, as well as geese, ducks and swans. There is a lovely view with Black Hill as the backdrop.

Continue on the track along the shore of Threipmuir for about 750m until you come to the dam and spillway. Keep to the path on the left, as the spillway can become treacherous with slippery algae and plant growth.

7 At the end of the spillway pick up the track as it follows the northwestern side of reservoir number five – **Harlaw** – again signposted to Harlaw Ranger Centre. Harlaw is a sharp contrast to Threipmuir – deeper, narrower, and surrounded by trees, mainly Scots pines. Still on the track, walk along for another kilometre, where you cross the spillway by a narrow metal bridge before walking along the top of the dam to **Harlaw House**.

Harlaw House is the former water-keeper's cottage, and now a visitor centre used by the Pentland Hills Ranger Service. There are displays and leaflets about the regional park, as well as a picnic area and toilet. The house is open daily, except Christmas Day and New Year's Day, although hours vary – check by phoning 0131 445 3383.

From Harlaw House keep on the metalled road until you reach a signpost by the double gates next to the car park (NT181654). From here take the track indicating Glencorse, as it heads southeast through **Maiden's Cleuch**. Keep on the track as it passes between fields, and after about 300m take the left fork at a junction signposted Glencorse.

Clubbiedean Reservoir from the west

Continue on the path, going through a gate, until you reach another gate and a signpost indicating Currie. Walk down this path towards a plantation and go through a gate. A rough, stony track continues for 1.5km to a white house at NT188667.

At the crossroads here turn right, following the SRWS sign to Torphin and Bonaly. Walk along the road, passing **Middle Kinleith** and then **East Kinleith Farm**. At East Kinleith go round a sharp bend to the right (follow the signpost indicating Bonaly and Torduff), in front of some cottages, to pick up the track as it leads to **Clubbiedean**. The track goes south, then after a bend, west.

Clubbiedean is also a good place for water birds, including dabchicks, mute swans, grey herons and cormorants.

8 Clubbiedean Reservoir is reached after about 800m. It has trees along its south banks and a unique character. ◄ Walk along the track, past a cottage at the east end of the reservoir. The track then crosses a narrow bridge before a gradual descent to another more substantial wooden bridge. Here there is a signpost to assist you, indicating Bonaly and Dreghorn.

9 The track becomes a metalled road after the wooden bridge by **Torduff Reservoir**, the final one of the round. Walking along the road, you overlook Torduff, a steep-sided, narrow body of water, with a feeling of remoteness belying its proximity to the city. The unfolding view of Edinburgh is also a lovely way to enjoy the end of the walk, particularly on a summer evening.

At the northern end of Torduff go through a gate and turn right, to walk along the fenced corridor on top of the dam, again signposted Bonaly and Dreghorn. At the end of the dam go through a wooden kissing gate and ascend some steps, at the top of which you pick up a narrow path heading around the base of Torduff Hill by a ruined fence. Keep on this path as it threads its way back to the car park and the start of the walk.

WALK 30
Robin's Round

Distance	13km
Ascent	350m
Time	3 hours 50 minutes
Maps	Ordnance Survey Landranger 66
	Ordnance Survey Explorer 344
Start/Finish	Swanston car park NT240674

1 The walk begins at **Swanston** car park, below Swanston village. From the car park walk back down the road to **Swanston Farm**, and then take a track to the left that leads past some livery stables.

This walk has a mixture of the skylines, views, wildlife and history. It is dedicated here to Dr Robin Aitken,

who loved the Pentlands and often did this walk. Robin became one of the first voluntary rangers, and was the founder and first chairman of the Friends of the Pentlands. Sadly, he passed away in January 2006.

Swanston Cottage, the house rented by Robert Louis Stevenson's parents in the summers between 1867 and 1880, is the large, whitewashed house on the right. Stevenson describes the house in *Edinburgh: Picturesque Notes*. The house was built in the 1760s for use by the city fathers for entertaining. It was enlarged in 1835, when a second storey was added, thatch was replaced with slate, and bow windows built. It is now a private residence. (See also Walk 2.)

Go along the track past the livery stables, with the tees, fairways and greens of Swanston Golf Course on the left, and the knoll of **Torgeith Knowe** (Gaelic *torr gaoithe*, meaning 'conical hill at the marsh') on the right.

2 The track eventually comes to **Long Plantation** (marked on OS 344), then turns sharp left uphill. Cross the wall ahead using the stone stile or the gate, and continue on the path by the trees that skirts the foot of the hill. The path crosses the burn that flows down **Smithy Cleuch**. (The word smithy comes from the Scots *smailly*, meaning 'narrow'.) ◄

3 Continue on until the path meets a number of other paths in a muddy area by **Green Craig Cistern**, a stone building used as a collecting point for water from surrounding springs. ◄ Follow the signpost here that indicates Castlelaw, taking the stony track that leads south and ascends gradually to the bealach between **Allermuir Hill** and **Capelaw Hill**. At the bealach the track is crossed by a path at NT223660.

4 Take this path to the right down through the heather, cross the dyke by the stile or gate, and contour round to the right (northeastern) side of Capelaw Hill.

5 The path curls round into a small rocky passage before swinging downhill and left (west) towards the trees around **Bonaly Reservoir**. At a gate and stile there is a signpost indicating Bonaly. Cross the stile and go down the track. Go through a gate and continue down the track until you leave the heather moorland at a gate by woodland.

You may come across small sandstone marker stones that indicate the line of the Bonaly pipeline. The one at NT228674 is badly damaged by gunfire from the now disused rifle ranges that used to be here.

Green Craig Cistern is dated 1790 and carved with the name Thomas Elder, Praefect (Lord Provost) – see Walk 3.

There are good views to be enjoyed from the track, and even in less clear weather the **Ochils** and **Lomond Hills** can be seen. The curlew, known locally as the whaup, nests on the moorland, and for me its prolonged, haunting call is the voice of the Pentlands. More prosaically, like many of our birds, it used to be valued as food. The largest of our waders, the female curlew may weigh 3lb, being the bigger sex and having a longer bill.

6 At the gate by the woodland there is a signpost – follow the post pointing to **Torduff Reservoir**. The path here goes along the top of the wood (known as Sanctuary Wood, but not shown on the map) and crosses **Blacklaws Burn** by a small bridge before reaching the southwest corner of the wood at NT207672.

At the kissing gate at the corner of the wood go left out onto the moorland, towards a wooden marker post, and take the path that descends down a grassy cleuch, which has been planted with trees, towards Torduff Reservoir. There is another kissing gate at the bottom of the path, and a signpost pointing to Bonaly and Dreghorn.

On a track, go in the direction indicated by the signpost, crossing the wooden bridge by the waterfall and joining the metalled road that skirts the western side of Torduff Reservoir. ▶ Go through a gate at the dam, next to the former water-keeper's house.

The city skyline unfolds before you, with Arthur's Seat and the castle prominent on the horizon.

Walk across the fenced top of the dam, which is signposted to Dreghorn. At the end of the dam go through a kissing gate and ascend some steps before contouring round to the left on a narrow path at the base of Torduff Hill. Keep on this path as it drops down in an area of gorse scrub to **Bonaly car park**.

Next to the car park is a sign pointing to Dreghorn. Take a narrow path as it leads into a shady cleuch, with a wooden bridge over **Dean Burn**. A few metres after crossing the bridge, the path divides. Take the left fork as it ascends steeply up the side of **White Hill**, keeping close to the perimeter fence of the Bonaly Scout Centre.

The path eventually drops down to a gate at NT216676. ◄ Go through the gate and strike out across the open field in front of you on a path under a line of electricity pylons. After about 500m you will reach a track where there is a signpost indicating Dreghorn. Continue on the track here, crossing a cattle-grid at the corner of a conifer plantation.

Much of this land used to be part of the **Dreghorn estate**, which included Dreghorn Castle. Built in 1658 by Sir William Murray, the castle had a succession of owners, including the Macfie family of sugar merchants. RA Macfie discovered the bones in the

The land here is Ministry of Defence property and used for army training. Be aware that there maybe troops on exercise and accompanying noise, etc.

Boundary stone damaged by gunfire

Cottages at Swanston village

Reindeer Cave (see Walk 2). The castle was acquired by the War Department in the early 20th century, but the burden of maintenance costs led to it being razed to the ground by 300 Parachute Squadron Royal Engineers on 1 May 1955.

7 Keep on the track as it passes the ruins of **Dreghorn Mains**, once the Dreghorn estate farm, until you arrive at a small car park next to the busy A720 Edinburgh City bypass. Walk to the far end of the car park and turn right on a track at the signpost pointing south to Castlelaw by Howden Glen, with the co-operation of the landowner.

A few metres from the signpost go through a kissing gate next to a field gate, and walk straight ahead through another gate as the path climbs very gradually to the left of a small copse of trees on a prominent knoll – **Chuckie Knowe**.

Beyond Chuckie Knowe take the path across an open grassy area, and just after fording a small burn go diagonally left (south) towards the trees of Long Plantation. On the south edge of the trees rejoin the path from your outward journey.

Go over the stone stile in the drystane dyke and retrace your steps to Swanston car park. If you have time, spend a while at Swanston village, enjoying the stillness.

APPENDIX 1
Route Summary Table

Walk		Distance (km)	Ascent (m)	Time (h/m)
1	A Capital View	5.5	390	2.00
2	In Stevenson's Footsteps	6	315	2.00
3	Hill, Moor and Wood	7	225	2.00
4	Three Reservoirs	9	214	2.30
5	A Phantom Walk	9	454	3.30
6	Harlaw Reservoir Circuit	3	0	0.45
7	Black Hill, Green Cleuch and Red Moss	8.5	125	2.20
8	Carnethy and Turnhouse	15	454	4.30
9	Three Peaks	13	484	4.00
10	Pentland Classic	17	457	5.00
11	Thieves' Road	27	484	7.30
12	West Linton and Siller Holes	10	80	2.40
13	Roman Road	14	110	3.40
14	Covenanters and Cairns	18	180	4.50
15	Walking with Wolves	15	465	4.35
16	Poets and Witches	8	185	2.20
17	North Esk Valley	7	210	2.10
18	The Monks' Road	6	215	1.50
19	The Four Tops	15	630	4.45
20	Carnethy 5	10	730	3.30
21	Carnethy Canter	6	294	2.00
22	History in the Hills	5	175	1.30
23	Flotterstone and Fala Knowe	8	230	2.25
24	Two Cleuchs	18	195	4.50
25	Pentland Tops	21	1210	7.15
26	Historical Hike	8	490	2.50
27	Exploring Caerketton	5	283	1.45
28	Find Your Way	8	390	2.40
29	Reservoir Round	20	275	5.30
30	Robin's Round	13	350	3.50

APPENDIX 2
Bibliography

Anderson, W *The Pentland Hills* W & R Chambers Ltd (1926)

Anon. *The Water Supply of Edinburgh, The British Waterworks Association* Edinburgh Corporation (1934)

Baldwin, JR *Exploring Scotland's Heritage* HMSO (1985)

Barnett, TR *Border By-Ways and Lothian Lore* John Grant Ltd (1944)

Cant, M *Villages of Edinburgh: An Illustrated Guide Vol. II* Malcolm Cant Publications (1999)

Cochrane, R *Pentland Walks with their Literary and Historical Associations* Andrew Elliot (1918)

Cocker, M and Mabey, R *Birds Britannica* Chatto and Windus (2005)

Crumley, J *Discovering the Pentland Hills* John Donald Publishers Ltd (1991)

Darwin, T *The Scots Herbal, The Plant Lore of Scotland* Mercat Press (1996)

Gordon, JE and Sutherland, DG (eds.) *Quaternary of Scotland* Chapman and Hall (1993)

Grant, W *The Call of the Pentlands* Robert Grant & Son (1927)

Grant, W *Pentland Days and Country Ways* Thomas Nelson and Sons Ltd (1934)

Harris, S *The Place Names of Edinburgh, Their Origins and History* Gordon Wright Publishing (1996)

Lawson, J and Truman, M *A Shepherd's Life* Scottish National Portrait Gallery (2000)

Loney, JWM *Notice of a group of long graves, stone-lined, near the source of the water of the North Esk* Proceedings of the Society of Antiquaries, Scotland Vol. 46 (1906)

Moir, DG *Pentland Walks, Their Literary and Historical Associations* John Bartholomew and Son Ltd (1977)

Morris, A and Bowman, J *The Pentlands' Pocket Book* Pentland Associates (1990)

Munro, I *The Birds of the Pentland Hills* Scottish Academic Press (1988)

Reith, GM *The Breezy Pentlands* TN Foulis (1910)

Smith, WA *The Pentland Hills, Their Paths and Passes* SROW and Recreation Society Ltd (1889)

Terry, CS *The Pentland Rising and Rullion Green* James Maclehose and Sons (1905)

Young, DM *Newhall* Edinburgh (1998)

APPENDIX 3
Glossary

Some of the words I have used may be unfamiliar to readers. A selection and their meanings are as follows.

bealach	a pass or saddle between two hills, sometimes termed a *col*
buchts	a collection of sheep pens
burn	a small stream
cleuch/cleugh	a ravine or narrow valley, from Middle English *cloghe*
coup	rubbish dump or midden
curlie doddie	devil's bit scabious or sheep's scabious
drystane dyke	a wall built without using mortar or cement
fank	a sheep pen
laverock	a skylark
march dyke	the boundary wall between two properties
noops	Northumbrian word for cloudberry
peewit	a lapwing
smiddy	blacksmith's workshop
stell	a drystane enclosure used for gathering sheep, usually circular and topped with turf
whaup	a curlew

NOTES

LISTING OF CICERONE GUIDES

BACKPACKING
Backpacker's Britain Vol 1 – Northern England
Backpacker's Britain Vol 2 – Wales
Backpacker's Britain Vol 3 – Northern Scotland
Book of the Bivvy
End to End Trail
Three Peaks, Ten Tors

BRITISH CYCLE GUIDES
Border Country Cycle Routes
Cumbria Cycle Way
Lancashire Cycle Way
Lands End to John O'Groats – Cycle Guide
Rural Rides No.1 – West Surrey
Rural Rides No.2 – East Surrey
South Lakeland Cycle Rides

CANOE GUIDES
Canoeist's Guide to the North-East

DERBYSHIRE, PEAK DISTRICT, EAST MIDLANDS
High Peak Walks
Historic Walks in Derbyshire
Star Family Walks Peak District and South Yorkshire
White Peak Walks Northern Dales
White Peak Walks Southern Dales

FOR COLLECTORS OF SUMMITS
Mts England & Wales Vol 1 – Wales
Mts England & Wales Vol 2 – England
Relative Hills of Britain

IRELAND
Irish Coast to Coast
Irish Coastal Walks
Mountains of Ireland

ISLE OF MAN
Isle of Man Coastal Path
Walking on the Isle of Man

LAKE DISTRICT AND MORECAMBE BAY
Atlas of the English Lakes
Coniston Copper Mines
Cumbria Coastal Way
Cumbria Way and Allerdale Ramble
Great Mountain Days in the Lake District
Lake District Angler's Guide
Lake District Winter Climbs
Roads and Tracks of the Lake District
Rocky Rambler's Wild Walks
Scrambles in the Lake District (North)
Scrambles in the Lake District (South)
Short Walks in Lakeland 1 – South
Short Walks in Lakeland 2 – North
Short Walks in Lakeland 3 – West
Tarns of Lakeland Vol 1 – West
Tarns of Lakeland Vol 2 – East
Tour of the Lake District
Walks in Silverdale and Arnside AONB

MIDLANDS
Cotswold Way

NORTHERN ENGLAND LONG-DISTANCE TRAILS
Dales Way
Hadrian's Wall Path
Northern Coast to Coast Walk
Pennine Way
Teesdale Way

NORTH-WEST ENGLAND
Family Walks in the Forest of Bowland
Historic Walks in Cheshire
Ribble Way
Walker's Guide to the Lancaster Canal
Walking in the Forest of Bowland and Pendle
Walking in Lancashire
Walks in Lancashire Witch Country
Walks in Ribble Country

PENNINES AND NORTH-EAST ENGLAND
Cleveland Way and Yorkshire Wolds Way
Historic Walks in North Yorkshire
North York Moors
South Pennine Walks
Yorkshire Dales – South and West
Walking in County Durham
Walking in the North Pennines
Walking in Northumberland
Walking in the South Pennines
Walking in the Wolds
Walks in Dales Country
Walks in the Yorkshire Dales
Walks on the North York Moors, books 1 and 2
Waterfall Walks – Teesdale and High Pennines
Yorkshire Dales Angler's Guide

SCOTLAND
Ben Nevis and Glen Coe
Border Country – A Walker's Guide
Border Pubs and Inns – A Walkers' Guide
Central Highlands: 6 Long Distance Walks
Great Glen Way
Isle of Skye, A Walker's Guide
North to the Cape
Pentland Hills: A Walker's Guide
Scotland's Far North
Scotland's Far West
Scotland's Mountain Ridges
Scottish Glens 1 – Cairngorm Glens
Scottish Glens 2 – Atholl Glens
Scottish Glens 3 – Glens of Rannoch
Scottish Glens 4 – Glens of Trossach
Scottish Glens 5 – Glens of Argyll
Scottish Glens 6 – The Great Glen
Scrambles in Lochaber

Southern Upland Way
Torridon – A Walker's Guide
Walking in the Cairngorms
Walking in the Hebrides
Walking in the Isle of Arran
Walking in the Lowther Hills
Walking in the Ochils, Campsie Fells and Lomond Hills
Walking the Galloway Hills
Walking the Munros Vol 1 – Southern, Central
Walking the Munros Vol 2 – Northern and Cairngorms
West Highland Way
Winter Climbs – Ben Nevis and Glencoe
Winter Climbs – Cairngorms

SOUTHERN ENGLAND
Channel Island Walks
Definitive Guide to Walking in London
Exmoor and the Quantocks
Greater Ridgeway
Isles of Scilly
Lea Valley Walk
North Downs Way
South Downs Way
South West Coast Path
Thames Path
Walker's Guide to the Isle of Wight
Walking in Bedfordshire
Walking in Berkshire
Walking in Buckinghamshire
Walking in Dorset
Walking in Kent
Walking in Somerset
Walking in Sussex
Walking on Dartmoor

UK GENERAL
National Trails

WALES AND WELSH BORDERS
Ascent of Snowdon
Glyndwr's Way
Hillwalking in Wales – Vol 1
Hillwalking in Wales – Vol 2
Hillwalking in Snowdonia
Lleyn Peninsula Coastal Path
Pembrokeshire Coastal Path
Ridges of Snowdonia
Scrambles in Snowdonia
Shropshire Hills – A Walker's Guide
Spirit Paths of Wales
Walking Offa's Dyke Path
Walking in Pembrokeshire
Welsh Winter Climbs

Cicerone's mission is to inform and inspire by
providing the best guides to exploring the world

Since its foundation over 30 years ago, Cicerone has specialised in publishing guidebooks and has built a reputation for quality and reliability. It now publishes nearly 300 guides to the major destinations for outdoor enthusiasts, including Europe, UK and the rest of the world.

Written by leading and committed specialists, Cicerone guides are recognised as the most authoritative. They are full of information, maps and illustrations so that the user can plan and complete a successful and safe trip or expedition – be it a long face climb, a walk over Lakeland fells, an alpine traverse, a Himalayan trek or a ramble in the countryside.

With a thorough introduction to assist planning, clear diagrams, maps and colour photographs to illustrate the terrain and route, and accurate and detailed text, Cicerone guides are designed for ease of use and access to the information.

If the facts on the ground change, or there is any aspect of a guide that you think we can improve, we are always delighted to hear from you.

Cicerone Press
2 Police Square Milnthorpe Cumbria LA7 7PY
Tel:01539 562 069   Fax:01539 563 417
e-mail:info@cicerone.co.uk   web:www.cicerone.co.uk

CICERONE